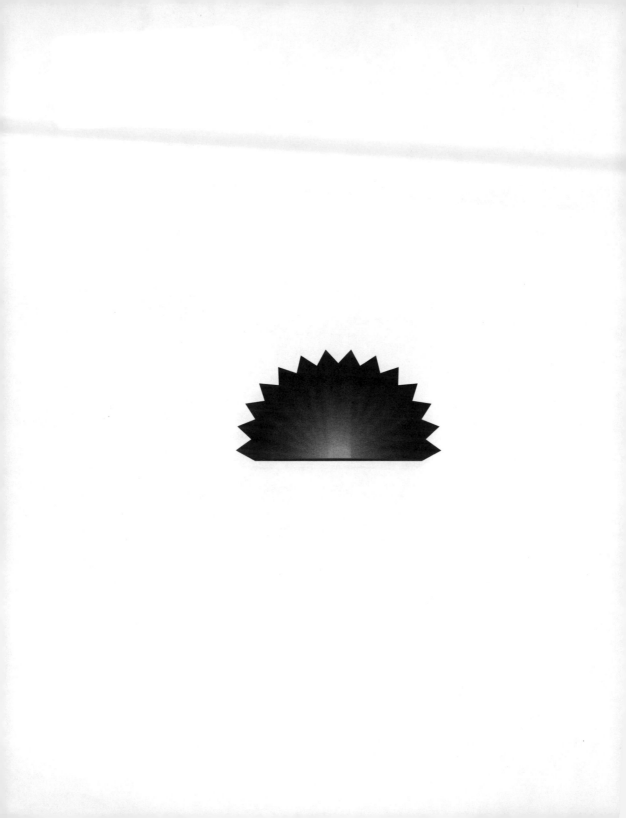

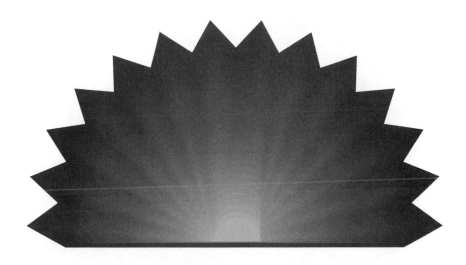

WHAT'S FOR BREAKFAST?

LIGHT & EASY MORNING MEALS FOR BUSY PEOPLE

Written by:
Donna S. Roy, MS, RD
Kathleen Flores, MS, RD

FIRST EDITION

APPLETREE PRESS, INC.
Mankato, Minnesota

Appletree Press, Inc.
151 Good Counsel Drive Suite 125
Mankato, MN 56001
Phone: (507) 345-4848
Fax: (507) 345-3002

Cataloging-in-Publication Data
Roy, Donna S.
    What's for breakfast?: Light and easy morning meals for busy people / Donna S.
Roy and Kathleen Flores ; foreward by W. Virgil Brown ; editors, Linda Hachfeld and
Faith Winchester.
    264p ; 21.6 cm
    Includes index
    Summary: What's for Breakfast? contains more than 100 recipes divided by time:
Super Quick to be done in 15 minutes or less; Quick in 30 minutes and Worth the Effort
for leisurely breakfasts and brunches. Each creative, light and easy recipes has nutri-
tional analysis and diabetic exchanges provided.
    ISBN 0-9620471-4-7
    1. Breakfasts. 2. Brunches. 3. Low-fat diet--Recipes. 4. Low-cholesterol
diet--Recipes. I. Flores, Kathleen. II. Hachfeld, Linda. III. Winchester, Faith.
TX733.R6 1994   94-072772
641.5'2--dc20

Editor: Linda Hachfeld
Assistant Editor: Faith Winchester
Artwork: Harlan Bloomer, Dan Gregoire and Michael Winchester
Cover Photography: Bill Badiner
Photo Stylists: Lisa Fechter and Linda Hachfeld

Cover: *Pizza Ramen-Ease Omelet* page 208, *Cafe au Lait* page 180,
Peach Smoothie page 92, *Appleberry Sauce* page 100,
Apricot Almond Spread page 102, and *Lemon Breakfast Cream* page 105.

Printed in the United States of America

ACKNOWLEDGMENTS

We would like to thank the following for their technical evaluation and support of the book:

Cindy Harris, MS, RD
Hortencia Mendoza-Martinez, MPH, RD

Sincere appreciation is felt toward those who read the manuscript and offered invaluable editing, critique, and support --

Editing:

Jeffery Roy - he was at the heart of the editing effort!!!!
Nancy Leich
Jerry Winston
Mary Hansen

Taste Testers:

Staff at the Rosenberg Dialysis Unit
Staff at the Lipid Research Clinic, Baylor College of Medicine

Data Handling:

Nancy Wang - her expertise in Word Perfect 5.1 was indispensable!!

DEDICATION

Lovingly dedicated to our parents, George and Milly Suzich, and Jimmy and Jerry Winston. Their understanding and support helped us overcome the many hurdles inherent in writing.

TABLE OF CONTENTS

TABLES

FOREWORD

Over 30 years ago, a group of scientists acting at the behest of the American Heart Association examined the relationship between what people ate in various countries around the world and the incidence of heart disease. They came to the conclusion that saturated fat and cholesterol components of animals in the various diets held the explanation for a rapidly advancing incidence of heart attack and stroke in Western Europe and the United States.

Post-war affluence and advances in the technology of food storage allowed the consumption of eggs, beef, pork and other hoofed animals at a level never previously consumed by the average man. This led the American Heart Association to make very specific recommendations for the reduction of saturated fat and cholesterol in our diet. To the amazement of many, the American people have listened to this message. Since the late 50's, there has been a steady reduction of these harmful components in the diet. There has been an equally steady reduction in the incidence of coronary heart disease in the U.S. and in other countries where similar dietary changes have been made.

The traditional American breakfast with its eggs, meat, butter and milk often contained more than half of the cholesterol and a large portion of saturated fat needed for the whole day. The disappearance of this traditional breakfast has served us well. Unfortunately, the usual reason for our abandoning this menu was not health consciousness but the busy lifestyle of the last quarter century. The authors of WHAT'S FOR BREAKFAST? have pointed out that there are many advantages to consuming a morning meal that can be quick, healthful and pleasurable.

This book goes far beyond simply providing new recipes for the first meal of the day. There is a wealth of information applicable to improving food choices at all meals. The simple, direct style makes this book easy to read and almost hides the sophistication of the factual material filling its pages. I believe that you will find this book a tremendous help in adopting the well-thought-out dietary recommendations of the American Heart Association. It could help you begin a better day while increasing the quality and number of those days.

W. Virgil Brown, MD
past president, American Heart Association
Professor of Medicine, Emory University
School of Medicine, Atlanta, Georgia

i

INTRODUCTION

Since childhood, we have been told that breakfast, particularly a healthy one, is our most important meal of the day. And exactly why is this so? The following reasons are convincing:

*   It prolongs life!

*   It helps shed unwanted pounds by controlling hunger!

*   It helps reduce the risk of heart disease!

*   It improves the overall quality of the diet!

*   It can help children do better in school!

Why do people either skip it, or choose less than nutritious foods? Generally, a person may be influenced by several short-term excuses:

"I don't have time to eat breakfast every day."
"I'm nauseated in the morning."
"I'm not hungry when I get up."
"I don't want to overeat."
"I only like doughnuts or bacon and eggs."

The chief intention in writing WHAT'S FOR BREAKFAST? LIGHT AND EASY MEALS FOR BUSY PEOPLE is to provide healthy meal tips that will encourage non-breakfast eaters to the breakfast table. For those with time constraints, the book contains recipes that can be prepared in 30 minutes or less, plus recipes that can be done ahead of time. Strategies to jump start morning appetites (like exercising and drinking less coffee) will steer readers down the road towards a more productive morning.

Some folks believe that eating breakfast makes them hungrier later that morning. This may be true, but it shows the body is working properly. It is perfectly normal to feel hunger 3-4 hours after eating a meal. So, if breakfast is taken at 8:00 am, you are bound to be a bit peckish by 12:00 noon. WHAT'S FOR BREAKFAST? will guide readers into making wise meal and mid-morning snack choices so that scavenging for doughnuts at 10:00 am becomes a thing of the past!

Many people have noticed that certain foods leave a hollow feeling in the stomach after only a couple of hours, like doughnuts or a sweetroll and coffee. When certain key nutrients are missing at breakfast, hunger creeps up much sooner than it should. A fundamental link to hunger control is the "pro-carb connection", an idea based on the fact that it takes sufficient amounts of carbohydrate AND protein at breakfast (with a bit of fat) to stay satisfied at least until mid-morning. Protein slows the digestion of carbohydrates, which in turn keeps blood sugar levels stable, ultimately providing control over your appetite as well as your weight.

Starting on page 74 are over 75 different pro-carb connection menus from which to choose. Each menu has at least one representative from the major food groups--milk and dairy, fruit and vegetable, bread and cereal, and meat. All menus provide 30% or less of their calories from fat. By furnishing an assortment of nutritionally balanced selections, the task of choosing just what to have for breakfast should be a little bit easier.

Don't get the idea that it is necessary to forever banish bacon and eggs from the menu. Lowering fat intake pays a hefty dividend--the ability to indulge regularly on what might be considered taboo. If every breakfast eaten Monday through Saturday is low in fat, there is nothing wrong with having bacon and an egg on Sunday. Then, only one of the seven breakfasts eaten that week would be considered high fat.

Food buying, and preparation techniques are fully outlined in WHAT'S FOR BREAK-FAST? "Shopping Guides" for brand name breakfast items will help fill refrigerators and pantries as well as nutritional requirements. Readers will learn how to change eating behaviors for a lifetime of healthy habits at EVERY meal.

The recipes starting on page 89 are compatible with the breakfast styles familiar to most Americans -- the quick morning meal for convenience. Check the following chapters on how to prepare fast and easy breakfasts:

Super Quick -- 15 minutes or less

Quick -- 35 minutes or less

Do Ahead recipes starting on page 177 accelerate
the preparation of muffins, biscuits, and other popular breakfast foods.
Worth the Effort recipes (over 35 minutes preparation time) fit in
with a more relaxed breakfast style, associated with weekend brunches
and special occasions. Use these recipes when time is not a pressing issue.

Recalling the mornings of your youth may bring back vivid memories of the smell of bacon sizzling, coffee brewing, and little hands rummaging for prizes inside cereal boxes. There is no reason why breakfast can't be just as enjoyable for adults and children of today. So, sit back and let WHAT'S FOR BREAKFAST? help recapture the joys of this marvelous and irreplaceable meal.

Donna S. Roy
Kathleen Flores
Houston, Texas

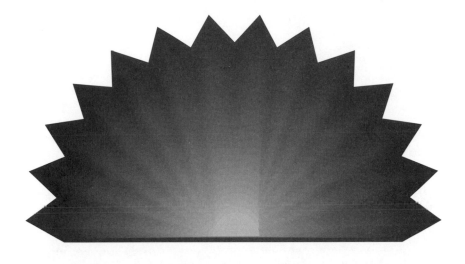

Why Breakfast?

Health is the thing that makes you feel that
now is the best time of the year.

Franklin P. Adams

Why Breakfast?

WHY BREAKFAST?

Studies show breakfast skippers encompass all age groups, but are most often 25 - 34 year old men and 15 - 24 year old women. Regardless of age or gender, breakfast is simply too important a meal to ignore. Here's why:

* Having breakfast is closely associated with a longer, happier life.

* Weight control is made easier.

* Cardiovascular disease risk is reduced.

* Nutrient intake is improved.

* School performance is enhanced (see page 45 in "Breakfast For Kids").

Live Longer and Happier with Breakfast

The breakfast habit has the honor of being part of an elite group of seven physical health practices that lengthen lifespans. People practicing six or more of these habits can outlive those who don't by up to 11 years [1]:

* Eating breakfast regularly (at least 4 times a week)

* Getting adequate rest

* Exercising regularly

* Not snacking, especially at night

* Maintaining a reasonable weight

* Not smoking

* Drinking alcohol in moderation (1-2 drinks a day)

Fatigue influences appetite. Tired people reach for whatever is handy.

Each of these habits relates to breakfast in one way or another. Adequate rest is very important because fatigue easily influences appetite and subsequent food choices. Tired people tend to reach for whatever is handy. Unfortunately, sugar, fats, and salt are the predominant ingredients in many convenience foods.

Both regular exercise and breakfast share a common bond; they promote a sense of well-being and facilitate weight control. If breakfast doesn't initially peak a person's interest, it will after exercise! Select an activity that is pleasurable and carry it out for at least 20 minutes every other day. Try a brisk walk, bike ride, or aerobics. Varying the activity (eg. swimming on one exercise day, then walking the next) will help sustain enthusiasm. Exercising with a partner can also bolster motivation.

Evening snacking inhibits morning appetite.

A quick note about evening snacking. It inhibits morning appetite. It may cause an overload of potentially empty calories at precisely the wrong time, with weight gain as the undesirable side effect. However, not ALL snacking leads to weight gain. Read more about breakfast's role in maintaining reasonable weight starting on page 6.

Smoking hampers appetite at just about every meal. It seems nicotine brings about a series of complex interactions in the central nervous system that obstruct hunger signals. Cigarette smokers also have lower blood levels of Vitamin C.

According to most health experts, one to two alcoholic drinks a day appear to have no deleterious health effects (except in pregnant women, who are advised to abstain). One drink is considered to be 1-1 1/2 ounces of hard liquor, 12 ounces of beer, or 6 ounces of wine.

Chase the Blues With Breakfast

Eating breakfast is related to a positive attitude.

In this high-stress society, feelings of anxiety and depression seem commonplace. Breakfast can improve psychological well-being, according to a study done in California by Wetzler and Ursano in 1977. Six thousand three hundred and twenty (6320) participants were given a health survey with questions about breakfast habits and general mood. There was a strong relationship between eating breakfast 3-7 times per week and positive attitudes of happiness and contentment regardless of age, sex, or educational level[2].

Breakfast restores blood sugar levels, reducing irritability, moodiness and fatigue.

Another study by Kawakami and colleagues reported in 1987 proved the same point. Over 3000 industrial workers responded to questionnaires about their mental state. Four health habits were directly associated with a lower incidence of depression. Eating breakfast (at least four times a week) is one of those habits. The other three are regular physical activity, moderate alcohol intake (1-2 drinks per day), and maintaining a desirable body weight[3].

Why breakfast improves mood and attitude isn't exactly clear. It is believed by some health authorities that blood sugar (glucose) plays a part in the scenario. Breakfast helps to replenish blood glucose levels, the brain's main energy source. Moodiness, irritability, and fatigue strike when levels are low, which often occurs by mid-morning. After a meal or snack, glucose values return to normal.

The Pivotal Role of Breakfast in Weight Maintenance

A characteristic pattern for many people with weight problems is skipping the morning meal, having a light lunch (or no lunch at all), and eating continuously from late afternoon through late evening.

Circadian Rhythm Theory: Hormones present early in the day cause the body to burn calories more efficently.

A vicious cycle begins when massive afternoon and evening meals are the norm. A person will be less hungry the next morning, bumping up the odds that breakfast will become a lost cause. This is grounds for concern, because food intake is lacking during a time of day when calorie burning could be most effective. Instead, food intake occurs during a time of day when calorie burning may be at its LEAST effective!

Why is this so? Many researchers have contemplated the reason, but there doesn't seem to be a clear cut answer. One hypothesis that has been studied reveals that hormones present early in the day cause the body to burn calories more efficiently. The actions of these hormones repeat themselves like clockwork. This pattern is referred to as a *circadian rhythm*.

Breakfast calories are burned more effectively than calories consumed later in the day.

To examine this phenomenon, a 1988 French study by Romon and colleagues looked at the effect of circadian rhythm on how the body burns calories from a meal. Nine men in the study ate three identical meals at 9:00 AM, 5:00 PM, and 1:00 AM. Activity levels of the participants remained the same throughout the trial. It was found that the burning of calories from the 9:00 AM meal was greater than with the other meals[4].

What health experts DO know for certain is the body actually heats up in the morning as it starts burning off breakfast calories. Bypass the meal, and warming up will take longer. Consequently, calories taken in later will be expended less efficiently. Compare the human body to an automobile engine on a cold winter morning and the food eaten as fuel. As the engine continues burning gasoline, it becomes more efficient. Without food, all the body has is a cold, lifeless engine.

The double whammy occurs when, after several hours of not eating, a person discovers that the tank is on empty. He then fills 'er up, thinking that all will be running smoothly. The analogy ends here though. Because he skipped breakfast, his metabolism has become quite sluggish. He loads up on calories, but his body will use them less efficiently. This is especially true later in the day, because he may be less active at this time. As a result, along comes something not particularly pleasant--weight gain!

Studies show that when daily calories are equal, breakfast consumers lose weight as opposed to dinner consumers.

Jacobs and colleagues demonstrated in 1975 that a single 2,000 calorie meal resulted in weight loss when eaten in the morning and weight gain if eaten at night[5]. French researchers reported in 1990 that 1312 over-weight subjects ate less calories in the morning but made up the difference by eating heavily at lunch and dinner[6].

To further strengthen the argument, Donna Roy conducted an informal survey of her overweight adult clients to determine how many ate break-fast. Not surprisingly, 30 out of 40 either just drank coffee or ate nothing at all.

In children, low or no intake of breakfast calories means higher body fat.

These findings hold true for children as well. France Bellisle and other French medical researchers surveyed the meal habits of 339 children ages 7-12. Obese and fat children ate less at breakfast and more at dinner. In short, low or no breakfast calories meant higher body fat[7].

Eating Breakfast May Lower Cardiovascular Risk

Balanced breakfast choices can provide a healthy edge in reducing total fat and dietary cholesterol. A survey of 4,000 households by General Mills, Inc. showed that adults who ate cereal for breakfast consumed fewer calories from fat throughout the day and 40% less cholesterol[8]. In 1989, Stanton and Keast from St. Joseph's University in Philadelphia reviewed data from the National Health and Nutrition Survey of 1977-1978 that studied dietary habits of over 11,000 participants. It was revealed that breakfast skippers had higher blood cholesterol than their breakfast-eating counterparts[9].

Adults who eat breakfast consume fewer calories from fat & less cholesterol throughout the day.

A well-respected study by Ken Resnicow from the American Health Foundation followed consumption habits of 530 school children ages 9-19 in 1991. Breakfast skippers had consistently higher blood cholesterol levels than cereal munchers[10].

Another exciting discovery is that when breakfast is eaten, blood clots are less likely to occur, thereby reducing the risk of heart attack and stroke. This accidental finding arose while researchers were studying a protein that reveals the degree of blood cell clumping or "sticking together." Twenty nine volunteers had this protein measured, once when they had eaten a 700 calorie breakfast, and again when breakfast was skipped. When the study group didn't eat breakfast, levels of the protein were 2 1/2 times higher, indicating a greater likelihood of clotting[11].

Breakfast Provides Much Needed Nutrients

Blood clots are less likely to occur in breakfast eaters than in breakfast skippers

Nutrients are defined as "those components of food necessary to sustain bodily functions" like breathing, muscular movement, and digestion. They include carbohydrate, protein, vitamins, and minerals. Given our abundance of food in this land, nutrient deficiencies shouldn't exist. Yet, the Nationwide Food Consumption Survey reveals that adequate calcium, iron, vitamin A and zinc are often missing from American diets[12]. Skipping breakfast is a contributing factor. The odds for meeting your nutritional needs increase when you eat three meals a day instead of only one or two.

The importance of carbohydrate and protein is provided in "The Breakfast Formula" (see page 74). Information on major vitamins and minerals needed for a healthy diet is discussed below followed by a review of

Skipping breakfast can lead to nutrient deficiencies.

nutrients that need to be moderated, namely, cholesterol, fat, and sodium. Last but not least, is a discussion about calories.

Vitamin Know-How

Vitamins and minerals are the invaluable elements gleaned from a good breakfast. For simplicity, this book focuses on those elements often deficient in our diets.

The word "vitamin" is derived from the word "vital," meaning essential for life. Without them (and zinc), the body could not convert carbohydrate, protein, and fat into useful byproducts. Nearly every body function is dependent on vitamins in one way or another.

There are two types of vitamins, fat-soluble and water soluble. Fat soluble vitamins (A, D, E, and K) can be stored in case of an emergency. Water-soluble representatives (B complex and C) can't be stored, so the body simply flushes out the excess through the urine.

Nutrients to increase: Vitamin A, Vitamin B Complex, Vitamin C, Vitamin E, Folic Acid, Calcium, Iron, Zinc and Fiber.

The first three letters of the alphabet are symbols of the mighty trio we know as vitamins A, B, and C:

Vitamin A improves vision in dim light and preserves normal skin tone. In the form of beta carotene, studies show it protects against the ravages of cancer, heart disease, and even cataracts.

The vitamin B complex (including niacin, thiamine, and riboflavin) boosts production of enzymes that initiate and sustain breathing, digestion, circulation, and other processes too numerous to mention.

Vitamin C, like A, also defends against cellular damage that can lead to any of the illnesses previously identified, and it also supports the integrity of the gums and skin.

Sadly, many of us consume insufficient amounts of vitamins.

The next two letters of the alphabet, D and E, represent a duo that share equal importance in the world of bodily activity. The body needs vitamin D so that calcium is absorbed into bones and teeth. It is sometimes called the *sunshine vitamin*, because ultraviolet rays transform a substance found in the skin into vitamin D. Since exposure to sunlight is seasonal for many people, there are laws which require milk to be "fortified" with vitamin D. Other rich sources are salmon and sardines.

Vitamin E, like vitamins A and C, neutralizes harmful substances that attack cells--a real trooper. Research is being done to see if supplemental doses of the vitamin can help prevent cancer and ease premenstrual syndrome (PMS). Vitamin E is found in polyunsaturated oils, margarine, and salad dressings (animal fats have no vitamin E). Deficiencies are relatively uncommon because the body can tap into vitamin stores when needed.

Sadly, many of us consume insufficient amounts of vitamins. This trend can easily be reverse by consuming more vitamin-rich fruits, vegetables, and dairy products. Breakfast is certainly a good a time as any to start. Eight fluid ounces of skim milk contribute riboflavin, and vitamins A and D. A 3/4 cup serving of berries or a piece of citrus fruit (oranges, grapefruit), provide 100% of your daily vitamin C needs.

This trend can be reversed by consuming more fruits, vegetables and dairy products.

A cup of cantaloupe chunks and one medium papaya each meet over two-thirds the recommended intake for vitamin A. By including a whole mango in the breakfast plan, a person receives sufficient vitamins A and C to meet daily recommended values.

The B-vitamins niacin and thiamine are found in common breakfast foods such as whole grains, bread, and cereal. These complex carbohydrates, along with skim milk and fruit, will provide substantial amounts of essential vitamins. Try them regularly for breakfast!

*Breakfast foods
are high in
vitamins.*

Folic acid (or folate) is a vitamin necessary for formation of red and white blood cells. Deficiency, often common in pregnant women, can cause anemia and neural tube defects in the infant. Dried beans and peas, berries, green leafy vegetables and fortified cereals are good sources.

Fiber

Whole grain breads and cereals provide another needed nutrient called fiber, which is the indigestible portion of plant foods that passes through the digestive system largely intact. It is no slouch, for during its journey many important tasks are fulfilled. Among these are proper bowel function, disease prevention, and weight control. How much total fiber is advocated for good health? The American Cancer Society encourages 20-35 grams per day. Besides whole grain products, other fiber sources include fresh fruits, vegetables, dried beans, and peas.

*Breakfast foods
are high in fiber.*

The average fiber intake in the U.S. is a mere 10-15 grams per day. The easiest way to pump up the fiber volume at breakfast is through whole grain cereals and fruit. A 1/2 cup of high fiber cereal such as All Bran® along with 1/4 cup sliced strawberries provides up to 50% of daily needs!

Avoid taking in much more than 35 grams of fiber per day. Valuable nutrients (specifically calcium and zinc) may get bound up with the fiber, thus preventing absorption in the intestines.

Many complain of intestinal gas and bloating when initiating high fiber diets. These problems should eventually subside. Regardless of whether or not these symptoms occur, it is best to begin gradually. One approach is to start eating a cereal with 3 grams of fiber per serving (see page 217). After 2-3 weeks, try one with twice this amount (or more if you wish).

Caution!
Increase fiber
gradually.

If you are eating a breakfast of convenience that is high in fat, the opportunity is missed to acquire beneficial nutrients. Compare the fiber, vitamin A, and vitamin C content of the following two menus:

Menu 1 will make it difficult to reach daily nutrient goals of 20-35 grams (gm) fiber, 800-1000 retinol equivalents (RE) vitamin A, and 60 milligrams (mg) vitamin C.

Menu 2 meets over 100% of the requirements for vitamin C, 50% vitamin A, and one-third the fiber.

Table 1: Menu Comparisons

	Fiber (gm)	Vitamin A (RE)	Vitamin C (mg)
Menu 1			
Sausage, egg, and biscuit sandwich	1	80	1.2
Coffee	---	---	-----
Totals	1	80	1.2
Menu 2			
1 ounce (1/4 cup) Grape Nuts®	3	370	2
8 ounces skim milk	---	149	----
2 waffles with syrup	4	100	----
1 glass orange juice	---	50	124
Totals	7	669	126

Source for Nutrition Information: Jean Pennington. FOOD VALUES OF PORTIONS COMMONLY USED, 16th edition. New York: J.B. Lippincott Co., Inc., 1994.

Minerals that Matter . . . Calcium

The mineral calcium works overtime by building strong bones, regulating heartbeat and transmitting nerve messages. Without it, the body breaks down bone that exists to replenish its supply. Women are especially vulnerable to this bone collapse, known as *osteoporosis*. Before things get this far, strive to meet these daily calcium recommendations:

* 400 to 600 milligrams for infants

* 800 milligrams for men, women, and children

* 1,200 milligrams for teenagers, pregnant, lactating, and post-menopausal women[13]

Breakfast can provide 1/3 of daily calcium needs.

Because dairy products are often consumed in the morning, breakfast offers the perfect opportunity to get one-third of the necessary calcium requirements. Cereal and milk, fruit and yogurt, or even a sandwich made with low-fat cheese are just a few of the ways to meet this quota. See Table 2 for best calcium food sources.

Milk has the same calcium content regardless of fat level. Calcium is not bound up in the milk fat, so it sticks around even when milk fat is removed. Plain yogurt has more calcium than the fruit-flavored variety and part-skim ricotta cheese contains more calcium than other cheeses.

If You and Milk Don't Mix

Some individuals, particularly as they age, develop problems digesting milk products. They experience discomfort due to a lack of the enzyme *lactase*, which digests the milk sugar lactose. Bloating, gas, abdominal cramping, and/or diarrhea are all too familiar symptoms. Coping with this

Table 2: Best Calcium Food Sources

Food Item	Calcium (milligrams)
1 cup milk (all types)	300
1 cup yogurt:	
plain	415
vanilla	390
fruit	315
1 oz. hard cheese (eg. American, cheddar, mozzarella)	200
1/2 cup part skim ricotta cheese	340
1/2 cup cottage cheese	70
1/2 c. green leafy vegetables*:	
(spinach, broccoli, greens)	80-100
Fish with edible bones:	
3 oz. salmon	170
3 oz. sardines	370
3 oz. shrimp	100

*Don't rely exclusively on green leafy vegetables for calcium. They contain compounds called oxalates which can inhibit absorption. This means that calcium passes through the body without being fully assimilated.

Source for Nutrition Information: Jean Pennington. FOOD VALUES OF PORTIONS COMMONLY USED, 16th edition. New York: J.B. Lippincott Co., Inc., 1994.

Lactase enzyme tablets help digest milk products for those who can't on their own.

problem is critical because milk is such a bountiful source of calcium. A smart tactic is to use lactase enzyme tablets which are manufactured by several companies including Lactaid® and Dairy Ease®. Taking one or two tablets before the dairy product is consumed converts the lactose before it reaches the intestine.

You can also "pre-treat" milk with lactase drops. The lactose is changed into a more digestible form before drinking. For added convenience, Lactaid® and Dairy Ease® now offer milk in the supermarket dairy case that has been commercially treated with lactase.

Calcium supplements can help meet calcium needs.

If milk or other high calcium foods still don't appeal, consider a calcium supplement. Antacids using calcium carbonate as their main ingredient (eg. Tums®) are suitable substitutes. Avoid brands that contain aluminum, which inhibits calcium assimilation.

Several years ago, Dr. Ralph Shangraw at the University of Maryland School of Pharmacy made a startling revelation regarding calcium supplements. Many don't break down completely enough in the stomach and small intestine to be fully absorbed. He now assures us that the situation is different today. Most brands checked recently have passed his tests with flying colors[14].

Use the "vinegar test" to determine supplement effectiveness.

If skeptical, evaluate the supplement with the vinegar test. Drop the calcium tablet into 3-4 ounces of vinegar. Stir it gently about every four minutes for half an hour. If the pill dissolves, it passes the test. If the tablet is still solid, return the bottle for a refund, and select another brand.

Information on Milk Intake

Milk is the first food of life, so let it be the first food of the day. A federal government publication entitled "Dietary Guidelines for Americans" advises that 2-3 servings daily of dairy foods become a habitual ritual. Reduced-fat varieties are preferable, and for good reason. They have fewer calories, cholesterol, and saturated fat, while still providing the same amount of protein, calcium and riboflavin. Welcome the day with at least one serving: (8 ounces) of skim, 1/2%, or 1% milk or yogurt[15].

Ease into low-fat and nonfat milk choices.

Changing from whole milk to the lower fat versions can be a turnoff for many people. Altered color and taste are the biggest complaints. To ease into the lighter stuff, drink 2% milk for a few weeks. One to two tablespoons of nonfat dry milk will fortify each cup with protein and restore that creamy white appearance. Be patient and before too long, the difference won't even be noticeable.

The switch to 1% milk can take place when tastebuds have gotten used to 2%, graduating to 1/2% or skim milk later. The benefit is the fat per cup drops to 0 grams for skim and .5 grams for 1/2% (as opposed to 3 grams for 1%). If the grocery store doesn't stock 1% or 1/2%, speak with the manager or write the local dairy council and request it.

For children 1-2 years of age, the calories from whole milk are still necessary for growth. Count on breast milk or formula before that, because babies can't effectively digest whole milk. After the age of two, they should drink the same lower fat milk as adults do.

Lowfat and nonfat yogurt are excellent breakfast options for non-milk drinkers. Try them with sliced fresh fruit and dry cereal, or make YO-GURT CHEESE (page 187) or LEMON BREAKFAST CREAM (page 105) for bagels and toast. The fat savings become quite apparent when comparing the amount per one tablespoon serving of yogurt cheese (0-2 grams) to the same quantity of cream cheese (5 grams).

Infants up to age 2 need whole milk.

Say Cheese

Ah, may America's love affair with cheese never die. But like most in-fat-uations, this one can be costly, for many whole milk types have 9-10 grams of fat per ounce. They are fine once or twice a week, one ounce per sitting--equivalent to 4 tablespoons shredded or an average slice. Shred-ded cheese is preferable to slices or cubes because a little bit goes further.

Most cooking applications are amenable to using shredded cheese (eg. sandwich making, omelet preparation, etc.).

Die-hard cheese lovers who refuse to be restricted to 2 ounces a week should consider light or fat-free versions. A list of those nationally available is on page 221 ("Shopping Guide": Recommended Cheeses), and highlights brands with 0-3 grams of fat per ounce, or no more than 2% fat by weight (for soft cheeses like cottage and farmer).

Look for cheese with 3 grams of fat or less per ounce.

Try to pass up cheese when dining out. Restaurants typically use large amounts of whole milk varieties, probably because not enough customers have insisted that low-fat cheeses be available for substitution.

Cream cheese, that delectable bagel spread, has been known to break fat budgets singlehandedly. Lighter ones like Weight Watchers® or Philly Light® brands cut the fat by 50% (if only reducing the federal budget was this easy!!!!). Equal parts light cream cheese and nonfat yogurt provides greater fat savings (70%). Fat-free cream cheese or YOGURT CHEESE (see page 187) goes one step further by providing 0 grams of fat per serving.

Iron Tidbits

Fat-free cream cheese is a good choice.

Iron is to blood as calcium is to bone. Without adequate iron, the formation of red blood cells is adversely affected. Too few red blood cells means oxygen fails to reach body tissues. Weariness and fatigue are the repercussions. As with calcium, the consumption of dietary iron is often inadequate in women. The recommended intake for menstruating and lactating women is 15 milligrams per day (pregnant women need 30 milligrams). Fortunately for adult men and most children, 10 milligrams is plenty (men 11-18 years of age need 12 milligrams per day).

Women need to consume more iron.

Most men have little difficulty reaching 10 milligrams every day because they ingest more food than women. More food means more iron is likely to be obtained. By the same token, women find 15 milligrams hard to achieve mainly because of lower calorie diets. An additional complication is that abundant iron is found in many cholesterol laden foods (eg. liver, beef, and egg yolks). Keep in mind, although these foods exact a higher cost in cholesterol, no single food is so totally "forbidden" that it should never be eaten.

For those having problems getting enough iron, all is not lost. Up to 30% of the daily allotment can be procured by eating iron- fortified wheat cereals several times per week, peanut butter (1-2 times per week), and egg yolks (3-4 times a week). Lean red meat can be enjoyed on a daily basis, as long as portion sizes are kept reasonable.

The presence of foods high in vitamin C maximizes the absorption of iron in the body. Optimal benefits are attained with the following food combinations (Foods high in vitamin C are capitalized). What follows are only some of the many possible combinations:

*   Leftover BAKED POTATO and two ounces lean roast beef (does this sound like last night's dinner? If so, it can taste just as good the next morning!)

Iron-fortified cereals can provide 30% of daily iron requirement.

*   A glass of ORANGE JUICE served with bran flakes and skim milk

*   Vegetable omelet made with 1 egg, 2 egg whites, and stuffed with   as much TOMATOES, GREEN PEPPER, and mushrooms as desired

Substances called *tannins* in coffee and tea may block iron absorption. Because of this, wait an hour after a meal before the first coffee break! Refrain from drinking coffee or tea before the meal because these beverages disrupt recognition of hunger signals.

Foods high in vitamin C maximize iron absorption.

Iron supplements are a good idea for pregnant women. Search for one that satisfies the recommended intake of 30 milligrams per day. There isn't a need to take much more than this amount, unless prescribed by a physician.

Table 3: Good Iron Sources

Food Item	Iron (milligrams)
2 ounces liver	4
2 ounces lean roast beef	2
2 ounces skinless chicken breast	1
1/2 cup pinto beans	2
1 ounce fortified bran flakes	8
1 tablespoon blackstrap molasses	3
1 egg yolk	1

Source for Nutrition Information: Jean Pennington. FOOD VALUES OF PORTIONS COMMONLY USED, 16th edition. New York: J.B. Lippincott Co., Inc., 1994.

Zinc Zingers

The senses of taste and smell, along with growth, skin tone, and immune function, all depend upon the action of zinc. This mineral is found in lean beef, liver, and seafood (especially oysters and shellfish). Because meat is so plentiful in our food supply, deficiencies are infrequent, but CAN happen. Meal skippers or low-calorie dieters are the prime targets[16].
The recommended daily zinc intakes are:

Infants	5 milligrams
Children 1-10 years of age	10 milligrams
Adult Males	15 milligrams
Females	12 milligrams
Pregnant Women	15 milligrams
Lactating Women	16-19 milligrams

Table 4: "Top 10" Foods Containing Zinc

Food Item	Zinc (mg)
Oysters, 3 ounces	76.0
Beef shank, 3 ounces	9.0
Chicken liver, 3 ounces	4.0
Raisin Bran cereal, dry 1/2 cup	1.5
Bran muffin, 1 medium	1.0
Baked beans, canned, 1/2 cup	1.0
Tofu (soybean curd), raw, 1/2 cup	1.0
Lowfat milk and yogurt, 1 cup	1.0
Green peas, 1/2 cup	.8
Flounder/halibut, 3 ounces	.5

Source for Nutrition Information: Jean Pennington. FOOD VALUES OF PORTIONS COMMONLY USED, 16th edition. New York: J.B. Lippincott Co., Inc., 1994.

Breakfast skippers may be deficient in zinc.

IMPORTANT NOTE FOR VEGETARIANS: Zinc from whole grains and soybeans is poorly absorbed by the body. Make it a point to drink plenty of skim or low-fat milk, because these foods contain readily absorbable zinc. Vegans (those that eat no meat at all) would more than likely need a zinc supplement.

Nutrition Nugget

Research shows that ready-to-eat cereal (RTE) and lowfat milk provide a way to get many of the essential nutrients just mentioned, while helping to reduce fat intake. Morgan and colleagues from University of Missouri

Eating cereal boosts iron, calcium, zinc and vitamin A intake.

and Michigan State University published a report in 1986 which observed that RTE cereals boosted daily intakes of iron, calcium, zinc, and vitamin A. In addition, both children and adult cereal eaters had less total fat and higher daily fiber intakes[17.]

A 1992 study conducted at Vanderbilt University by Schlundt and colleagues substantiates Morgan's study results. Fifty two (52) moderately overweight women were selected for participation. Those that didn't eat breakfast were instructed to do so (the meals were 400 calories worth of cereal and/or muffins).

After six months of breakfast eating, the proportion of calories coming from fat dropped nearly seven percentage points (from 38% to 31%). During this same period, percentage of calories from carbohydrate rose from 43% to 46%. Why their fat intake decreased is another interesting facet to this study. Having breakfast helped prevent the subjects from impulsively munching on high fat snacks later in the day[18.]

Sample Breakfast Plans
For Getting A Head Start
On Major Vitamin And Mineral Needs

* 6 fluid ounces orange juice
  1/2 cantaloupe
  1 slice whole grain toast with 1 tablespoon peanut butter
  8 fluid ounces skim milk

* 1 whole mango
  whole wheat bagel with 2 tablespoons fat-free cream cheese
  8 fluid ounces skim milk

* 3/4 cup oatmeal with sliced banana and 1/2 cup sliced berries
  6 fluid ounces apricot nectar
  8 fluid ounces skim milk

* 1 kiwifruit
  1-2 ounces cereal (see page 217)
  with 1 tablespoon wheat germ sprinkled on top
  8 fluid ounces skim milk

* 1 cup bran cereal (like Raisin Bran®, Bran Flakes®, etc.)
  1-2 cups skim milk
  1/2 banana
  1/2 grapefruit

Cholesterol Concerns

If any single term in nutrition can be accused of having a double meaning, cholesterol is it. Much confusion revolves around this odorless, soft, waxy substance. Strictly speaking, cholesterol is needed for cell development and the production of hormones and vitamin D. About 30% of what is in the body comes from the food we eat. The remainder (70%) is produced internally by the liver. Therefore, more than twice as much comes from your own body than from your diet[19].

Nutrients to moderate include cholesterol, fat, saturated fat, sodium, and calories.

The double meaning mentioned earlier has to do with the differences between total *blood* cholesterol versus *dietary* cholesterol.   Blood cholesterol encompasses what the liver produces PLUS the dietary cholesterol. The recommended total blood cholesterol level is 200 milligrams (mg) or less per deciliter (dl) of blood. Higher levels indicate an increased risk of heart disease.

The two major components of total blood cholesterol are low density lipoprotein (LDL) and high density lipoprotein (HDL). LDL is the "bad" guy that builds up in the bloodstream and leads to heart problems. This level should be below 130 mg/dl. HDL acts as the "good" guy by hunting down the LDL and carrying it back to the liver for disposal. A desirable level is at least 35 mg/dl.

Dietary cholesterol is found in the lean part of meat.

Dietary cholesterol comes only from the food you eat. Basically speaking, any food that comes from an animal contains cholesterol. Its presence is restricted to egg yolks, animal flesh, organ meats, shellfish, and dairy products. Interestingly enough, cholesterol is found in the lean portion of the meat, not the fatty part. So, regardless of how much fat is trimmed, the cholesterol remains.

In and of themselves, fruits, vegetables, grains, and oils have no cholesterol. They should only be a concern to the cholesterol conscious when combined with eggs, dairy products, or meats.

Numerous studies have proven that too much dietary cholesterol and saturated fat stimulate the liver to generate a glut of total blood cholesterol. When this occurs, excess amounts enter the bloodstream in the form of LDL and lead to the development of plaque in the arteries. This *plaque* is composed of fatty deposits that attach to blood vessel walls and accumulate over time. These deposits narrow the blood passageways, making it increasingly difficult to supply vital organs with oxygen, including the heart. Lack of oxygen kills heart cells, causing a heart attack.

Blood cholesterol comes from food we eat and what our liver manufactures.

Intakes of cholesterol should be 300 milligrams or less per day, which can be achieved by:

*   Limiting meat portions to 6 ounces a day, with no more than 1-2 ounces at breakfast.

To decide whether or not a food has cholesterol, keep this motto in mind: "If you can pull it from the ground or pluck it from a tree, it doesn't have cholesterol."

* Reducing the number of egg yolks to no more than 4 a week (egg whites and egg substitutes can be eaten as often as desired)

* Opting for shellfish no more than 1-2 times a week and organ meats once a month.

* Using nonfat or lowfat dairy products (milk, yogurt, and cheese) instead of whole milk products.

Information on Egg Intake

Ever wonder why eggs are universally popular at breakfast? Ancient folklore purported that when eggs are eaten upon awakening, a revitalization of the body and spirit occurred. Due to egg's versatility, taste, and cost, they are often a regular breakfast food.

Medical experts have been telling us for the last 20 years not to eat so many eggs. It is often overlooked that yolks are what need to be restricted, not whites. An average sized whole egg has 5 grams of fat and 213 milligrams cholesterol. But as with all foods, even yolks have their place in a fat/cholesterol conscious society. The American Heart Association guidelines permit 3-4 a week.

"Wait a minute!" you say. The recommended daily cholesterol goal is 300 milligrams or less. How can 213 milligrams of cholesterol fit into one day and leave room for other cholesterol-containing foods? The answer is to not think of a single day--look at the entire week. There are 2100 milligrams of cholesterol that are allowed every seven days (300 x 7 = 2100). Four egg yolks comprise less than half the total (213 x 4 = 852). Reserve the greater half for those small portions of meat, 1-2% milk, cheese, and butter that will cross your palate. Using fewer than four egg yolks a week allows even more flexibility in meal planning.

Have as many egg whites as desired--they contain no fat or cholesterol. Substitute two whites for each egg yolk in any recipe. Many a diner has been served a yolkless omelet that tasted outstanding!

Eggs are a good food choice. Limit egg yolks to no more than 4 a week.

Don't be concerned with eggs used in the preparation of most baked goods. Foods with large amounts of egg, like quiche (1 small piece, or 1/8 of a 9 inch pie), French toast (1 slice), or custard (1/2 cup), however, are a entirely different matter. Every serving you eat counts as one egg yolk unless the recipe is modified with egg whites or egg substitutes.

Purchase egg substitutes with one gram or less of fat a serving (See "Shopping Guide": Egg Substitutes, page 227). A personal favorite is Fleischmann's Eggbeaters®. It produces very tasty omelets and French toast, and works well in most baking recipes calling for whole eggs. Swap 1/4 cup of substitute for every whole egg.

A Word About Raw Eggs

Caution! Do not eat raw eggs or prepare in-the-shell in the microwave.

Raw eggs have recently been linked to outbreaks of food poisoning from a type of bacteria called salmonella enteritidis. Improper handling at warehouses and during transit is implicated in the majority of cases. Buy eggs that are refrigerated and not displayed at room temperature. Always store eggs in your refrigerator at or below 45 degrees Fahrenheit and eat within two weeks of purchase. Cook eggs until the white is set and the yolk has thickened around the edges.

Avoid cooking eggs in the microwave with their shells on. Because of the intense heat that builds up inside the egg as it cooks, there is a good chance it can explode, resulting in burns to the face and hands.

Fat Facts

Rather than a lengthy discussion on the scientific definition of fat, let's instead focus on reviewing its role in the body. Besides making food tasty and filling, fat insulates and protects internal organs, maintains nerve, brain, and spinal cord function, and assists the body's absorption of vitamins A, D, E, and K.

Fat calories are more likely stored as body fat.

Fat also contributes the highest concentration of energy from food at 9 calories per gram (carbohydrate and protein yield 4 calories, alcohol gives off 7). As with protein, fat can be utilized as an energy source during dieting or exercise after glycogen runs out. Since fat contains over twice the energy of carbohydrates and proteins, fat calories are even more likely to be stored as body FAT.

According to national surveys, Americans eat roughly 37% of their calories as fat (previously, it was 42%, so we are improving!). The recommendations set by the National Cholesterol Education Program (NCEP) are 30% or less total calories from fat[20].

Fat percentages in diets of other cultures (see Table 5, next page) vary greatly, and are closely linked with what makes up the bulk of their meals[21].

Eat 10-30% of total daily calories from fat.

People often ask, "How low can my daily fat percentage go?" The minimum is 10% of total daily calories from fat. One might ask why the fat percentage recommended by NCEP isn't set closer to the minimum requirement (10%). Because of the quantities and types of food available in this country, it would be very difficult for most people to cut back to this degree immediately. As people learn to modify their habits, the current goal could be reduced in the future. According to several studies, the 30% level helps lower blood cholesterol and still allows flexibility in meal planning. Fat intake can be lower than the recommended goal, but just make sure it is at least 10% of total calories (see Appendices C & F, pages 247 & 252, for reviews on estimating caloric and fat requirements).

The type of fat can be as important as the total amount. There are three types to be acquainted with--saturated, polyunsaturated, and monounsaturated. Pay very close attention to the saturates because of their negative effect on heart health.

Table 5: Fat Intakes of Other Countries

Country	Percent of Calories from Fat	Major source of dietary fat
China	15%	Little meat, plenty of starch
Japan	15-20%	Ditto, but fat intake is climbing due to Westernization
Britain	43%	Lots of eggs, butter, and meat
Russia	50%	Huge amounts of sausage, bacon, solid pork fat
Norway	36%	Mainly because of meat
France	37%	Cheese and meat
Italy	32%	Meat consumption has increased fourfold since 1950!
Switzerland	42%	Due to, what else, meat!

Saturated Fat Facts

Because of the media's preoccupation with cholesterol, many people are not aware of the role saturated fats play in the onset of coronary heart disease. Through a complex process, they prompt the liver to generate excess cholesterol, which contributes to plaque development in the arteries. Trimming back saturated fat and cholesterol intake can slow and possibly reverse this process. According to NCEP, no more than 10% of

Saturated fat prompts the liver to generate excess cholesterol.

the total calories or less than 1/3 of your daily fat should come from saturated fats (see page 254 for help in estimating saturated fat gram intake).

Lard, butter, and tropical oils (coconut, palm, palm kernel, and cocoa butter) are saturated fats added to foods during processing or cooking. Because of a powerful consumer push, the use of tropical oils in commercial food products has diminished. Saturated fat does still lurk within many breakfast favorites, such as egg yolks, sausage, bacon, whole milk products, doughnuts, croissants, and pastries.

Purely saturated fats are solid at room temperature. On your next supermarket visit, look at coconut oil and notice how "firm" it is in its natural state. Food manufacturers can also recreate this texture through a process called "hydrogenation," or "partial hydrogenation," which converts a previously polyunsaturated oil into shortening. Longer shelf life and a velvety texture are the major reasons for the conversion.

Saturates also exist naturally in most liquid oils. Two grams of saturated fat per tablespoon is the recommended upper limit for an oil. For a more extensive listing of oils and their saturated fat content, see Table 6.

Polyunsaturated Oils

One-third of daily fat calories should be polyunsaturated.

Polyunsaturated fatty acids (PUFAS) are derived from plants like corn and soybeans, and are found primarily in a liquid state. The grains or seeds are usually heated and pressed in such a way that the oil in them is extracted. When considering which oil to buy, check to see that the specific grain or vegetable source is identified in the title (eg. corn, soybean, etc.). A brand calling itself "vegetable oil" may contain too much saturated fat (more than 3 grams per tablespoon serving).

Moderate consumption of PUFAS can decrease blood cholesterol when substituted for saturated fat. However, too much can lead to a drop in HDL, or the "good" cholesterol. To avoid this, no more than 1/3 of your total fat intake should be polyunsaturated oils.

Table 6: Saturated Fat Comparison

A listing of fats in order of saturated fat content (lowest to highest)

Select oils with 2 grams or less of saturated fat per tablespoon.

Oil (1 tablespoon)	Saturated Fat (g)
Canola Oil	1
Safflower Oil	1
Sunflower Oil	2
Corn Oil	2
Olive Oil	2
Soybean Oil	2
Peanut Oil	3
Cottonseed Oil	4
Lard	6
Palm Oil	8
Beef Tallow	8
Butterfat	10
Coconut Oil	14

Monounsaturated Oils

Walnut oil and peanut oil are examples of monounsaturated fats.

Monounsaturated fats include olive, peanut and canola oils. All are liquid at room temperature, and are excellent replacements for saturated fats. Monounsaturates should constitute the remaining 1/3 of daily total fat intake (recall that 1/3 should come from saturates and the other 1/3 from polyunsaturates). Nuts such as walnuts, peanuts, and almonds are also good sources of monounsaturated oils.

Table 7: Recommended Unsaturated Oils

Polyunsaturated Oil	*Partial List of National Brands*
Corn	Mazola, Crisco, Lou Ana, Hain
Soybean	Wesson Vegetable
Sunflower	Wesson
Safflower	Hollywood, Hain
Sesame	Hain

Monounsaturated Oil	*Partial List of National Brands*
Canola	Crisco Puritan, Wesson, LuAnna, Hollywood, Mazola Right Blend
Olive	Bertolli, Pompeian, Progresso, World Classics

A Quick Word on Canola Oil . . .

Canola oil has the lowest saturated fat content of any oil.

Canola oil has an unusual name and the lowest saturated fat content of any oil (1 gram per tablespoon). It is derived from the rapeseed plant, a member of the mustard seed family. Canada influenced the selection of its name ("Can") because the plant was first discovered there. Any brand of canola oil is acceptable so long as the word "canola" is identified on the label.

Dietitians are often asked, "Which cooking oil is the best?" In terms of saturated fat content, canola is the lowest. This doesn't mean that the other oils are unacceptable, for each has its place in the kitchen. Olive oil is wonderful in pasta and marinades, but a strong taste prohibits its use in baking. The absence of a discernible flavor means canola oil will complement just about anything.

In short, feel free to alternate oils as desired, but watch the quantity when preparing recipes. Remember that measuring is the only way to know just how much fat is entering your diet from these sources.

Trans-lating Trans-Fatty Acids

Trans-fatty acids found in some stick margarines can elevate total and LDL cholesterol.

Is margarine really preferable to butter? It depends on the TYPE of margarine. When liquid unsaturated oils like corn and soybean are hardened (or partially hydrogenated) for "spreading" purposes, their molecular structure changes. This new arrangement is called a "trans" configuration. It has been discovered that trans fatty acids are responsible for elevations in total and LDL ("bad") cholesterol. A study of 748 men at Harvard Medical School in Boston by Troisi, Willett, and Weiss revealed a 27% increase in the risk of heart disease when trans fatty acid intakes went from 2.1 to 4.9 grams per day[22].

Why blood cholesterol responds unfavorably to trans fatty acids is a mystery at this writing. Consumer reaction to the news was one of bewilderment, with some people renouncing margarine and going back to butter.

Choose margarines which are labeled "saturated fat free."

Currently, there is no information for trans fatty acid content listed on margarine labels. What you can be sure of is that if a food is listed as "saturated fat free," it is not supposed to contain more than half a gram of trans fat.

How should we deal with this dearth of information? Until more studies are conducted, it is prudent not to abandon margarine and go back exclusively to butter, which is almost totally saturated fat. There are acceptable margarines available! Here are a few tips on how to locate them:

Choose a margarine with an unsaturated oil listed first on the label.

* First check the total fat content on the nutrition label. Margarine with less than 8 grams of fat per tablespoon serving are on the lighter side, and will mean less total fat regardless of what type of oil is used. Just watch those portion sizes (no more than a teaspoon per slice of bread, pancake, waffle, etc.)!

* Next, examine the ingredient label for the type of oil(s) contained within. You will find that many spreads have both liquid unsaturated and partially hydrogenated oil. What's printed first is present in the greatest quantity. Make sure a liquid unsaturated oil is listed before its partially hydrogenated "alter ego."

* Consult the margarine guide on page 229 for brand-name recommendations for stick, tub and squeeze margarines.

Sodium Smarts

Today's most plentiful mineral was once a form of currency in the ancient world. As a matter of fact, the word salary comes from the Latin term for salt, *salaria*! For centuries, it was a universal means of preserving meat and other perishable items. With the advent of refrigeration, salt was used less as a preservative and more as a flavoring agent.

The most notable characteristic of sodium is the ability to maintain "water balance" in the body. It acts like a "sponge" to absorb excess fluid that isn't needed by the tissues. Too much salt upsets this delicate balance and can increase pressure in the arteries. Many people simply excrete surplus salt through their kidneys. If they cannot, high blood pressure (hypertension) ensues. Those with a strong family history of hypertension are especially susceptible, including many African-Americans.

Notice the interchange of the words "sodium" and "salt," even though they aren't quite the same. Sodium is often found combined with another element to form one of several different compounds. Sodium chloride (table salt), is 40% sodium and 60% chloride. Other sodium compounds commonly used in food preparation include sodium bicarbonate (baking soda), monosodium glutamate (MSG) and sodium nitrite.

According to a study at the Monell Chemical Senses Center in Philadelphia, the majority of sodium in the typical American diet (75%) comes from processed foods. Many traditional breakfast foods, like sausage, ham, and canned biscuits have more than 300 milligrams per serving. Salt added during cooking and at the table accounts for 15% of sodium eaten. Sodium occurring naturally in food and drinking water makes up only 10% of the total[25].

From childhood, our palates have grown accustomed to the taste of salt due to its appearance in a plethora of foods. As with fat, people tend to go overboard. One-eighth of a teaspoon (.5 gram) per day is all that is necessary. The average American unwittingly digests 20 times that much! For most of us, our bodies get rid of the excess, but some people have a problem doing so. This is why the American Heart Association recommends no more than 3,000 milligrams per day.

The majority of sodium (75%) in our diets comes from processed foods.

If a person has high blood pressure, he should pay close attention to the sodium content of foods with more than 140-160 mg of sodium per serving. Observe the two breakfast menus in Table 8 (see next page) and note the marked differences in sodium content.

To lessen added salt in cooking and at the table, rely on salt substitutes and herb blends available at the market. Popular salt substitutes include Papa Dash® and No Salt® brands. Savory herb blends found in many spice sections include Mrs. Dash®, Accent Salt Free®, Parsley Patch®, and Lawry's Salt Free®.

Note: When deciding on a salt substitute, one should see a doctor before making a selection. Some have large amounts of potassium that is contra-indicated with certain antihypertensive medications.

Table 8: Sodium Breakfast Comparisons

High Sodium Breakfast		Low Sodium Breakfast	
Food	Sodium (mg)	Food	Sodium (mg)
4 fluid ounces tomato juice	243	4 ounces orange juice	1
2 fried eggs	288	3/4 cup shredded wheat	trace
2 slices bacon	200	8 ounces skim milk	126
2 slices white toast	246	2 slices wheat toast	246
2 teaspoons margarine	92	2 teaspoons margarine	2
1 tablespoon jelly	trace	1 tablespoon jelly	trace
1 cup black coffee	2	1 cup black coffee	2
Total	1071 mg	Total	377 mg

Source for Nutrition Information: Jean Pennington. FOOD VALUES OF PORTIONS COMMONLY USED, 16th edition. New York: J.B. Lippincott Co., Inc., 1994.

Calorie Care

What exactly is a calorie? It is defined as the amount of energy in the form of heat found in all foods. Food contains heat? Yes! Here is how it works. During digestion, certain nutrients (carbohydrates, proteins, and fats) are released from food. They fuel the body's furnace, so to speak. The energy produced is used for life sustaining activities such as breathing, muscle movement, and cell production. Calories are even "burned" when eating, which is why it helps to have at least three balanced meals a day, especially breakfast!

More calories taken in means more energy is accessible. This energy either gets burned to keep the "furnace" going OR is turned into body fat. If caloric intake equals the amount of energy expended, present weight is maintained. If caloric intake is higher than the energy expended, the extra calories are stored as body fat, leading to weight gain. If caloric intake is lower than what is being burned, weight loss results as the body digs into its fat reserves. The following statements will help you retain the basic concepts:

When	You Have
Caloric Input **EQUALS** Calories Burned	Weight Maintenance
Caloric Input **GREATER THAN** Calories Burned	Weight Gain
Caloric Input **LESS THAN** Calories Burned	Weight Loss

See the Appendix, page 247 to estimate caloric requirements.

Breakfast is the most important meal of the day.

To summarize the best of all possible breakfasts . . .
Here in a nutshell,
Are 10 things to know
from WHAT'S FOR BREAKFAST?
the book that helps breakfast wisdom grow.
It's all been tied together,
In hopes that all can see,
How simple and rewarding
Changing breakfast habits can be!

Breakfast Summary

Ten Important Points

* No doubt about it--breakfast IS the most important meal of the day.

* There is no room in a healthy diet for a "good" food, "bad" food mentality. Any food can fit into a properly planned breakfast pattern.

* Have a nutritious breakfast EVERY DAY.

* Monitor the fat content of food to help cut down on unnecessary fat calories.

* Emphasize MORE carbohydrate, moderate amounts of lean protein, LESS fat.

* Identify those nutrients that may be deficient in your diet and use breakfast as a starting point for turning things around.

* Don't think of "diet" as deprivation; instead, think of D.I.E.T. as Developing Intelligent Eating Techniques that last a lifetime.

* Variety prevents boredom and enhances nutrient availability.

* Become an effective label reader who concentrates on the major concepts and doesn't get bogged down with unnecessary details (see Appendix, page 254).

* Teach healthy eating habits to children EARLY so they can effectively carry them over into adulthood.

The Breakfast Philosophy

There is No Such Thing as a "Good" Food or a "Bad" Food

The assumption persists that a food must fall into either the "good" or "bad" category. This means that it can be eaten anytime OR should be avoided altogether. The impression that certain foods must be eliminated can only lead to feelings of deprivation. Denying yourself the pleasure of eating a favorite food is a form of self-punishment that won't permit positive eating behaviors to develop[24].

In moderation, anything can fit into a healthful diet.

In moderation, anything can fit into a healthful diet. For example, two doughnuts each and every morning is excessive. They have too much fat and too little nutritional value. When lower fat and more nutritious foods are eaten most of the time, a doughnut once or twice a week is a reasonable luxury.

The best way to understand the concept of moderation is to look at what you eat in the space of a few days or a week. If you splurge at a Sunday morning brunch, remember it is only one out of the many meals you will be having the next 3-7 days. Subsequent meals that are lower in fat and higher in fiber can offset those from earlier in the week.

Variety is the Spice of Breakfast

Beat breakfast boredom with variety.

Many people don't realize they have the same 3-4 foods for breakfast over and over again. No wonder boredom rears its ugly head! There is incredible variety available--the time has come to challenge the tastebuds. The shopping guides and recipes in WHAT'S FOR BREAKFAST will help break breakfast monotony.

Never Say "Diet"

Diet: Regularly consumed foods

Diet is defined in Webster's Dictionary as "a food or drink regularly consumed." The words "sacrifice" and "deprivation" are never mentioned! So, where did people get the crazy idea that a diet is a temporary avoidance of all the foods we love? We needn't GIVE UP anything -- just learn to MODERATE intake of high fat foods and INCREASE intake of low fat, nutritious ones.

A sound diet means enjoying all foods either in moderation or with some modifications to lower fat and cholesterol content.

A colleague from Boston, Miriam Erick, M.S., R.D., came up with this acronym: D.I.E.T., which stands for DEVELOPING INTELLIGENT EATING TECHNIQUES, a smart way to stay healthy.

Remember That We Are Unique Individuals -- What Works For One May Not Work For Another

Diet does not mean sacrifice, punishment or weight loss.

Most weight loss programs fail because they champion a rigid "diet" for their clients without bothering to individualize the meal plan. A person must adopt an eating style that's right for them. If a morning pastry is just too difficult to pass up, look for other things that CAN be changed. It may be easier to cut back on high fat spreads, coffee creamers, or breakfast meat.

Change Habits Gradually

Time and time again, dietitians see people who want to radically alter meal patterns straightaway. They go from doughnut, coffee, and fried egg orgies to dry toast and orange juice rations. Why the rush? Overnight conversions are doomed because the body hasn't had time to adapt. Think of the first day at a new job. It can seem so overwhelming. We want to learn everything instantly and perform with perfection, but our good intentions may falter when we realize the magnitude of the task. Slowly but surely, we get used to the new surroundings and things start falling into place.

Gradual changes are permanent.

The same is true when modifying dietary habits. If your goal is more cereal, toast, juice and milk and less eggs, sausage, and hash browns, the road ahead may seem a little daunting. Instead of doing an immediate about-face, start off by skipping the sausage and eating the hash browns, eggs, and toast. Let a couple of weeks pass, then switch from white toast to whole wheat. Then take another step forward and substitute cereal for the hash browns.

Remember this is not a race. Take some time so the adjustments last. Gradual changes are more permanent.

Individuals Can Make Change Happen

Only you can make change happen.

The decision to embark on this lifelong journey toward better breakfasts can be made by only one person--the person involved! No amount of coaxing by anyone else will do. Their efforts will be successful once one realizes the primary purpose of food is fuel for the body. Its secondary role is emotional satisfaction, and not the other way around.

The best opportunity to acquire positive eating behavior is in our youth. Be a good role model. Eating habits developed during childhood have the potential to last a lifetime. Children "learn" good eating habits from others. If children omit breakfast, they will most likely continue this "habit" into adulthood.

Notes

[1] C.A. Schoenborn, "Health Habits of U.S. Adults, 1985: The 'Alameda 7' Revisited." PUBLIC HEALTH REPORTS 101 (1985): 571-580.

[2] H.P. Wetzler, R.J. Ursano, "A Positive Association Between Physical Health Practices and Psychological Well-Being." THE JOURNAL OF NERVOUS AND MENTAL DISEASE 176 (5) (1988): 280-283.

[3] N. Kawakami, et al. "Relationship Between Health Practices and Depressive Mood Among Industrial Workers." JAPANESE JOURNAL OF INDUSTRIAL HEALTH 29 (1) (1987) 55-63.

[4] M. Romon, et al. "Circadian Variation of Diet-Induced Thermogenesis." AMERICAN JOURNAL OF CLINICAL NUTRITION 57 (1993): 476-480.

[5] A.G. Caviezel, et al. "Single Daily Meal Treatment in Obesity." Serono Symposium No. 28, London: Academic Press, 1981.

[6] J. Fricker, et al. "Circadian Rhythm of Energy Intake and Corpulence Status in Adults." INTERNATIONAL JOURNAL OF OBESITY 14 (5) (1990): 387-393.

[7] F. Bellisle, et al. "Obesity and Food Intake in Children: Evidence for a Role of Metabolic and/or Behavioral Daily Rhythms." APPETITE 11(2) (1988): 111-118.

[8] General Mills Nutrition Department Ten-Year Nutrient Intake Study Report. "Breakfast Perspectives." Minneapolis, 1991.

[9] J.L. Stanton, D.R. Keast, "Serum Cholesterol, Fat Intake, and Breakfast Consumption in the United States Adult Population." JOURNAL OF THE AMERICAN COLLEGE OF NUTRITION 8(6) (1989): 567-572.

[10] K. Resnicow, "The Relationship Between Breakfast Habits and Plasma Cholesterol Levels in Schoolchildren." JOURNAL OF SCHOOL HEALTH 61(2) (1991): 81-85.

[11] R. Cifcova, et al. "Platelet Activation is Increased After Overnight Fasting and Decreased After Meal." The National Conference on Cholesterol and High Blood Pressure

Control Abstracts, page 151.

[12] U.S. Department of Agriculture, Human Nutrition Information Service. NATION-WIDE FOOD CONSUMPTION SURVEY. Springfield, Va: National Technical Inforation Service, 1991.

[13] L. Bean, "Calcium Sources: Some Considerations." DAIRY COUNCIL DIGEST. May-June 1989: 14-18.

[14] Joe Graedon, The People's Pharmacy. HOUSTON CHRONICLE, November 19, 1991: C8.

[15] U.S. Department of Agriculture, Human Nutrition Information Service. DIETARY GUIDELINES FOR AMERICANS. Home and Garden Bulletin No. 232-11, 1989.

[16] L.D. McBean, ZINC IN HUMAN NUTRITION National Live Stock and Meat Board/Beef Promotion and Research Board, 1991.

[17] J. Morgan, et al. "The Role of Breakfast in Diet Adequacy of the U.S. Adult Population." JOURNAL OF THE AMERICAN COLLEGE OF NUTRITION 5 (1986): 551-563.

[18] D. Schlundt, et al. "The Role of Breakfast in the Treatment of Obesity: A Randomized Clinical Trial." AMERICAN JOURNAL OF CLINICAL NUTRITION 55 (1992): 645-651.

[19] Peter Kwiterovich, BEYOND CHOLESTEROL. Baltimore: The Johns Hopkins University Press, 1989.

20 Expert Panel on Detection, Evaluation, and Treatment of High Blood Cholesterol in Adults. REPORT OF THE EXPERT PANEL ON DETECTION, EVALUATION, AND TREATMENT OF HIGH BLOOD CHOLESTEROL IN ADULTS. Bethesda: National Heart, Lung, and Blood Institute, 1993.

[21] Euronut SENECA Investigators. "Intake of Energy and Nutrients." EUROPEAN JOURNAL OF CLINICAL NUTRITION 45 (Suppl. 3): 105-119.

[22] R. Troisi, W.C. Willett, and S.T. Weiss, "Trans-Fatty Acid Intake in Relation to Serum Lipid Concentrations in Adult Men." AMERICAN JOURNAL OF CLINICAL NUTRITION 56 (1992): 1019-1024.

[23] R. Mattes, D. Donnelly, "Relative Contributions of Dietary Sodium Sources". JOURNAL OF THE AMERICAN COLLEGE OF NUTRITION. 10 (1991): 383-393.

[24] S. McNutt, "Diet, a Dirty Word?" THE HEARTY APPETITE NEWSLETTER. Summer, 1990.

Breakfast
for Kids

Breakfast makes good memory.

————

Rabelais

Breakfast For Kids!

Breakfast for Kids!

Breakfast is just as important for kids as grown-ups, maybe even more so. Children can leave home without eating and not feel so much as a tummy growl, but their lack of nourishment will eventually overtake them. The reaction to hunger is more pronounced in little bodies as they require more calories per pound of body weight.

Young people will tire more quickly and have increased difficulty performing physical and mental tasks.

It is disconcerting to realize that over 44% of kids ages 8-13 skip breakfast regularly[1].

In a 1987 report by Meyers and colleagues called CCHIP (the Food Research and Action Center's Community Childhood Hunger Identification Project), children who skipped breakfast tended to score lower on tests that involved problem solving and expressing thoughts. These results were especially noticeable in children who were malnourished and in low socioeconomic groups.

When a breakfast consisting of milk, juice, toast, and/or cereal was given to these students, grades on the annual standardized achievement test improved in subjects like language, reading, and mathematics[2].

Children's overall nutrition also improves with breakfast. Researchers affiliated with the renowned Bogalusa Heart Study at Louisiana State University discovered that

children who ate breakfast had a much better chance of meeting their daily requirements.

Kids who skip breakfast have higher blood cholesterol levels than those who eat breakfast.

Skippers missed out on as much as two-thirds the recommended daily allowances for many vitamins and minerals (calcium, phosphorus, magnesium, riboflavin, vitamin A, vitamin B-12, and folic acid)[3].

To determine if improvements in nutrient intakes would have any effect on blood cholesterol, researcher Ken Resnicow studied 532 middle and high school students from New York and Atlanta. Based on the results of a breakfast habit checklist, each child was categorized into one of six food groupings: 1) chronic skipper, 2) RTE (ready-to-eat) cereal with fiber, 3) traditional breakfast, 4) chips or sweets, 5) other non-fibrous RTE cereals, and 6) mixed breakfasts (eg. bread, fruit, and/or coffee).

Those in Group 1 that disregarded breakfast did indeed have higher blood cholesterol values than anyone in Groups 2-6. Higher body weight, greater fat, and lower fiber intake were just a few of the other characteristics that the kids in Group 1 seemed to have in common[4].

Despite the rewards, time constraints and disinterest often make it difficult for kids to have breakfast. The solution is found in strategies allowing more time in the morning, identifying nutrition basics for children, and dealing with picky or indifferent eaters.

Devoting Time to Children's Breakfast

Breakfast needs to become a top priority by planning for it.

It is often difficult to get children to have breakfast because of time constraints. Between waking the family, exercising, taking a shower, shaving, dressing, feeding the dog, brewing the coffee, reading the paper, and packing lunches, breakfast is often given low priority. With all these activities, no wonder it ends up on the "back burner."

Six tips to help you find time for breakfast.

The best recourse is planning beforehand:

1. Start initial breakfast preparation the night before. Let kids set out the bowls, plates, spoons, napkins, cups, and glasses that will be used. Also try prepacking lunches and school bags.

2. Depending on what is being served the next morning, here are some other time-trimming suggestions to do the night before: making juice, defrosting meat and egg substitute in the refrigerator, mixing pancake or french toast batter, baking muffins or coffee cake, washing and slicing fruit, or placing cereal boxes on the table.

3. Freeze the many healthy muffins, waffles, and pancake recipes found in WHAT'S FOR BREAKFAST for use at a later time. Simply remove from the freezer and defrost in the microwave for 30-35 seconds.

4. Pick out what clothes everyone will wear the next day. Have those 4 years and older choose their outfits and instruct them to dress upon awakening.

5. Set the alarm 15 minutes earlier than usual. The extra time can make all the difference between a frenzied or relaxed meal.

6. Keep the T.V. off so it doesn't cut into dressing or eating time. Let this be the household motto: "No Barney or Sesame Street until breakfast is over."

Now that the time crunch has been alleviated, more attention can be devoted to breakfast.

School Breakfast

Many public schools offer breakfast.

If eating at home just isn't in the cards, check out the breakfast program at your neighborhood school. The Food Research and Action Center (FRAC) launched the National School Breakfast Expansion Campaign in 1987 in an effort to recruit, educate, and counsel breakfast organizers across the country. Today, nearly 37,000 schools nationwide offer breakfast programs, reaching a total of 4 million children daily. A federal subsidy allows schools to provide nutritionally balanced breakfasts either on a reduced cost basis or free to those from low-income families.

Breakfast at school is a good deal, both economically and nutritionally.

If youngsters aren't getting fed at home, parents have the responsibility to see that the educational system fills the gap. School breakfast doesn't have to be expensive--cereal and lowfat milk will suffice. Every child deserves to attend a school that has a breakfast program.

These are publications from FRAC that can help get a school breakfast program started:

"Fuel for Excellence"

"Breakfast: Don't Start School Without It!"

To receive more information, write to:
Food Research and Action Center
1875 Connecticut N.W. Suite 540
Washington, DC 20009

Children need protein to grow and carbohydrate for energy.

Special Nutrient Needs for Children

What do children do better than most grownups? Besides getting into mischief, growing right out of their clothes and always looking for something to eat are two things that come to mind. A constant supply of protein and carbohydrate, with a modest dose of fat, will keep the pep in their step.

Those growth spurts that seem to happen overnight are made possible by "Protein" and its conversion to body tissue. Its faithful sidekick "Carbohydrate" supplies energy. Together, their breakfast mission is fighting off hunger until lunch comes to the rescue. Find these good buddies in the following food groups[5]:

Children need 1-2 servings each of protein and carbohydrate at breakfast.

Protein Sources	Carbohydrate Sources
Meat, Fish, Poultry	Fruits and Vegetables
Eggs and Egg Substitutes	Bread and Cereal
Dried Beans and Peas	Dried Beans and Peas
Milk, Yogurt, Cheese	Milk, Yogurt, Cheese
Nuts and Seeds	

Children should be eating one to two servings each of a protein and carbohydrate food at breakfast. Portion sizes should be adjusted based upon the age of the child. For a good overview of portion size recommendations, refer to Ellyn Satter's book HOW TO GET YOUR KID TO EAT...BUT NOT TOO MUCH[6].

Note: Don't give nuts or seeds to small children until they can chew and swallow them properly.

Protein and Carbohydrate Combinations for Children

Serve all meals with milk and 100% fruit juice.

* Peanut butter and jelly on bread (whole wheat at least 1/2 the time if possible).

* 1-2 slices of a cheese pizza

Children, especially pre-schoolers, will need a mid-morning snack.

* Hot dog (For breakfast? Why not, so long as it's no more than once or twice a week.) Go for the 97-98% fat free dogs and whole wheat hot dog buns.

* Make egg salad with 1/2 a chopped boiled egg mixed with 1 tablespoon light or fat-free mayonnaise, then spread on their favorite bread.

Any of the breakfast tacos, burritos, sandwiches, or pizza recipes nestled within the recipe section of WHAT'S FOR BREAKFAST? (See recipes in the "Super Quick," "Quick" and "Worth the Effort" sections).

More kid's menu ideas can be found in "The Breakfast Formula," starting on page 74.

For very young children (ages 2-6), plan for a morning snack containing adequate protein and carbohydrate, since their stomachs often can't hold enough to last the 4-5 hours until lunch.

But What About Fat?

Children over age 2 can follow fat recommendations as for adults.

According to the National Cholesterol Education Program (NCEP), children over 2 years of age have the same dietary goals for fat as adults do (30% of total calories).

Some parents go overboard with this recommendation and reduce their child's fat intake to inadequate levels way below the 30% goal. Realisti-

Use higher fat foods as occasional foods, not as everyday foods.

cally, the 30% recommendation won't jeopardize their growth or take the enjoyment out of eating.

Children need to recognize high-fat foods as a treat rather than an everyday routine. To get around their objections, gradually introduce low-fat foods while occasionally allowing bacon, sausage, or a doughnut. This will set them on a course towards healthier eating as adults. As part of this gradual introduction, experiment at home with low-fat ingredients as in this book's muffin, biscuit, pancake and French toast recipes, as well as the CINNAMON CRISPS WITH APPLESAUCE (page 135).

Let kids know how important nutritious foods really are, especially for breakfast. Grades will improve, morale will skyrocket, and more energy will be available for their morning classes. However, don't try bribing a child into eating something that is healthful.

Putting the Calcium in Nutritious Kid Breakfasts

Simply put, calcium-rich diets make the bones and teeth of children stronger and more "dense." Get that milk container ready for pouring, because hidden inside a 1 cup serving is 300 milligrams of calcium providing 38% of the daily demand for 2-10 year olds and 25% for adolescents.

Dairy products are rich in calcium as well as protein.

If tykes consider plain milk "gross," lowfat chocolate milk and flavored milk drink mixes may be easier to swallow. Though the sugar content is higher, it is far better than going without milk entirely. Some doctors say that chocolate in milk hinders calcium absorption and suggest it be avoided. Scientists at this point aren't really sure how much, if any, calcium is affected. The best advice is to go ahead and serve the chocolate milk anyway. Better to try getting some calcium than none at all.

A bounty of calcium is also present in yogurt. While most children turn their noses up at the plain or unsweetened varieties, those with fruit, nuts, or colored sprinkles are often accepted without complaint. Check out the recipes in the "Super Quick" section for yogurt sundaes, various fruit shakes, smoothies, and coolers.

Look for cheese with 3 grams of fat or less per ounce.

Cheese also plays the role of calcium contributor in award-winning fashion, as a one ounce serving delivers 25-30% of the recommended daily allowance. Let children sample some low-fat or fat-free varieties (0-3 grams of fat per ounce) and decide which ones best please their palates. Cheese is a food for all ages and can be enjoyed melted over toast, English muffins, or folded into biscuit dough (see recipe for SPEEDY CHEDDAR BISCUITS on page 148). Part-skim mozzarella cheese is available in individual packages and makes for a marvelous finger food with crackers and apple slices. Kids' eyes will light up when offered a slice of leftover cheese pizza and juice!

If a child dislikes all milk products, try calcium-fortified juices. Keep in mind however, that these beverages don't offer any protein or the B vitamin riboflavin. To provide a decent supply of these two nutrients, accompany the juice with foods like enriched breads served with low-fat cheese, or a wholesome cereal.

Relief for children who can't tolerate dairy products.

For those that are lactose intolerant, add lactase enzyme to milk or buy brands that are already pre-treated (see page 14). On the other hand, beware of abdominal pain, vomiting, diarrhea, runny nose, or skin rashes. These are common symptoms of an allergic reaction or sensitivity to milk (as well as other possible food culprits). Contact a pediatrician should these symptoms occur.

Iron for Kiddies

Children need between 10 and 15 milligrams of iron every day for normal blood cell development. Where does much of their iron come from? Surprisingly, the answer is ready-to-eat cereal! One serving can satisfy up to 25-35% of the daily recommendation.

Tots young and old should also be served lean meat, fish, or poultry regularly to make up the difference in iron. Child feeding expert, Ellyn Satter, suggests that if toddlers drink two cups of milk a day, one ounce of meat a day will provide the balance of iron needed. Serve two ounces of meat daily to preschoolers and three ounces for the school-age child. With the onset of puberty, these figures rise to 3-4 cups of milk and four ounces of meat a day. If a child doesn't eat meat, refer to the text on protein complementation on page 66.

Many fruits and vegetables are renowned for their abundance of vitamins A and C. Since vegetables usually aren't at the top of a youngster's wish list at breakfast, keep the peace by offering some of these sweet tastin' fruits every morning:

For vitamin A	For vitamin C
Apricots (fresh, dried, or nectar)	Oranges and grapefruit (fresh, canned, or juice)
Cantaloupe	Cantaloupe
Mango	Mango
Kiwifruit	Kiwifruit
Nectarine	Papaya
Purple plums	Berries

Because the nutritional content is virtually the same, it doesn't matter if the fruits are fresh, canned, frozen, or dried. If whole, uncut fruit is difficult for your child to handle, serve it sliced for dipping into peanut butter, yogurt, or the PEANUT BUTTER CREAM, found in the "Super Quick" section (see page 106).

What to Do About Picky Eaters

Establish meal routines that fit your family.

Unfortunately, one of the more exasperating aspects of parenting begins at meal time. Some parents are too authoritative with food, and think they should command exactly what and how much should be eaten. Children may feel their independence is being compromised and will rebel by doing just the opposite. Other parents can be too permissive, with no established feeding structure whatsoever. Without some sort of a fixed routine, breakfast may never become a daily event.

Seek the middle ground by adopting a firm, yet flexible feeding policy. According to Ellyn Satter, two fundamental rules will make feeding your children less stressful[7]:

Two rules for making mealtimes less stressful . . .

Parents are responsible for what is presented to eat and the manner in which it is presented.

Children are responsible for how much and even whether they eat.

Parents should try to not be deterred by tantrums or criticism that may occur once their expectations are known. Grown-ups can respond to complaints but not be browbeaten into forsaking their basic feeding guidelines.

Here are some basic guidelines to handle picky eaters:

*   Give children some options from which to choose.

This can be as simple as whether cereal is served hot or cold, or what topping goes on a waffle. Asking a question like "What do you want for breakfast?" may be answered with "I don't know," or "I don't want anything." Instead, say something like, "Do you want pancakes or a yogurt sundae?" Let them make the choice.

If they want something else that isn't very healthy, be flexible. There are times when serving something is better than having them skip breakfast entirely. Even if the reply is "Just a doughnut," it is better than nothing! Be ready to offer something healthier later in the day.

Picky Eater
Guildelines:
* give children
*   options*
* revise/modify
*   recipes*
* involve children
*   in the kitchen*

*   Should the family be yearning for something novel, sift through
     health, cooking, or parent magazines.

Revise recipes to your heart's content. We mean this literally! If a recipe is suspected to be too fattening, lighten it up (see "Recipe Modifications" on page 232). Oftentimes, other ingredients can be substituted for ones that are too expensive or just don't sound appetizing. For instance, when the recipe calls for fresh raspberries, use frozen berries or canned fruit instead.

*   If "breakfast" stands for "boring" in junior's vocabulary, involve
     him/her in its preparation.

A child can end up feeling like a real household helper. An added incentive is the opportunity to spend some extra time together. Read cooking instructions aloud first, then demonstrate each step in language your little one is able to grasp. Next, match cooking tasks with skill and/or age level. For example, three and four year olds can open cereal boxes, beat eggs with a fork, and pour milk, while five year olds can assist in preparation of pancake batter, hot cereal, or French toast. Practice the recipe a few

WHAT'S FOR
BREAKFAST?
recipes that "fit"
children well.

times before allowing the little chef to go solo. Always be nearby in case a helping hand is needed.

Several "child-friendly" recipes are found in WHAT'S FOR BREAK-FAST and can easily prepared by kids 9 years old and up. Younger kids can still engage in such steps as spreading toppings on bread, cracking eggs and peeling bananas.

To further stimulate interest, parents may want to assign regular kitchen duties, like toasting the bread and pouring the juice. A little help is worth its weight in gold on busy mornings. Be sure to teach kids the fine art of cleaning up as they cook.

Children learn from watching adults.

*   Be a role model and eat with your child.

We can't expect children to cultivate the breakfast habit without a commitment on our parts to do the same. Having breakfast every day means children are more likely to follow their parents' lead. Kids tend to imitate adults, so if the parents aren't eating, neither will the kids.

*   Unless you want to pave a path toward overeating, DON'T force children to "clean" their plates, especially with threats of punishment or promises of reward.

Let children decide when to stop eating. Don't encourage overeating.

We are born with easily recognized indicators of when we have had enough to eat. The need to comply with parental wishes can easily interfere with a child's perception of these indicators. What happens is an increased risk of eating for reasons other than satisfying hunger. Unwanted weight gain may be the unwelcome result. A parent's job is to serve the food, but let the child decide when to stop eating.

*   What if the child simply won't come to the table, period!?

Late evening meals or snacks can discourage breakfast eaters.

It could be she just isn't hungry. There must be some reason for this, so start probing into nightly eating habits or juice drinking before breakfast. Late evening meals after 8:00 pm are notorious for keeping morning appetites at bay. Serving dinner a little earlier should remedy the situation, especially for teenagers who are notorious night feeders and breakfast skippers!

The first thing many kids want after awakening is juice. It is not uncommon for them to go through upwards of 24 ounces a day! This most assuredly deadens the desire for food. Resist giving juices on demand before breakfast and serve water instead. With especially fussy eaters, start offering half-strength juice (50% water, 50% juice), then graduate to plain water after a few weeks. If a lack of appetite continues for more than a few days and results in poor growth, weight loss, fatigue, or skin pallor, talk with a pediatrician.

Blueprints for Breakfast Fun

Fun ideas for the breakfast table.

Want to know the secret of keeping kids hooked on breakfast? It's all in the presentation. Children love celebrating special occasions, playing games, and learning new things. There is no time like the present to liven things up!

*   Try festive placemats designed for children. On holidays, use holiday napkins and candles.

*   Play guessing games about what will be served, allowing three choices.

*   Blindfold the child and have him "feel" a mystery food in order to guess what it is.

*   Write up a simple "Wheel-of-Fortune" style puzzle with the answer being a type of food.

*   If you are making something with toppings, let kids assemble ingredients and serve themselves.

*   Buy waffle irons and pancake pans in fun shapes, like stars, hearts, and footballs.

*   Plan an unconventional morning birthday party complete with such delicacies as BREAKFAST PIZZA (page 123), YOGURT SUNDAES (page 98), and BANANA BOATS (page 96).

*   Take into account the seasons of the year. Hot cocoa is a fine winter warmer. Bring fresh flowers to the dining area come springtime. For fall, take advantage of the annual apple crop by garnishing breakfast plates with fresh apple slices. Keep a bowl of fresh fruit on the table regardless of season!

Create amusing figures and shapes with fruit, like the following:

Breakfast ideas for tots and young children.

Clown Face: On a plate, use 2 kiwi slices for the eyes, maraschino cherry for the nose, and a small banana sliced lengthwise for the mouth.

Red Caterpillar: Cut 3 strawberries of equal size in half, and line the six pieces across the plate, cut side down. Press two whole cloves in the first half for the eyes (remove cloves before serving).

Peter Cottontail Pear Bunny: Lay a canned pear half flat side down on a small plate. Use two almonds for the ears, a maraschino cherry for the mouth, and a dollop of light whipped topping for the tail.

Orange Flower: Take a small peeled orange and separate the segments about half the way down. Press a small strawberry in the center.

Catch the holiday spirit with these attention getters:

Holiday breakfast ideas.

New Year's Day: Black-eyed peas are a New Year's symbol of good luck in the South. Make quick black-eyed pea nachos by processing 1/4 cup canned, drained, black-eyed peas until smooth, and spreading it on toast. Sprinkle with shredded light cheddar cheese, and chopped tomatoes.

President's Day: FRUIT PIZZA (see page 113) using cherry pie filling.

Valentine's Day: Heart-shaped cutouts from pancakes or waffles topped with sliced strawberries and light whipped topping.

St. Patrick's Day: Put green food coloring in apple juice or milk.

Easter: Decorate the breakfast table with colored Easter eggs and 3-4 pear bunnies (directions above).

July 4: Place tiny toothpick flags in breakfast sandwiches, muffins, etc.

Halloween: Name foods after ghostly characters (eg. orange juice with blue food coloring/witches brew, chocolate milk/devil's drool, graham crackers/ghoulish grahams, scrambled eggs with red food coloring/monster mush, etc.). For Jack-o-Lantern fruit bowls, cut the top off an orange. Scoop out the inside. Using a marker, draw a jack-o-lantern face outside the orange. Fill with mixed fruit.

Thanksgiving: Whip up pumpkin muffins or bread.

Christmas: Hot cocoa with candy cane stirrers.

Suggested books with children in mind.

The book CREATIVE FOOD EXPERIENCES FOR CHILDREN by Mary T. Goodwin and Gerry Pollen (Center for Science in the Public Interest, 1980) is an excellent resource for additional ideas. Any recipes contained within can be modified to be lower in fat when appropriate.

Other suggested books include:

CHILD OF MINE, FEEDING WITH LOVE AND GOOD SENSE and HOW TO GET YOUR KID TO EAT...BUT NOT TOO MUCH by Ellyn Satter, R.D. (Bull Publishing, 1986, 1987)

KITCHEN FUN FOR KIDS by Michael Jacobson, PhD and Laura Hill (Henry Holt and Company, 1991)

BEST KIDS COOKBOOK (Sunset Publishing, 1992)

ONCE UPON A RECIPE by Karen Greene (Putnam Publishing, 1992)

Notes

[1] "Power Breakfasts for Kids." PARENTING Sept. 1994: 176-177.

[2] A.F. Meyers, et al. "School Breakfast Program and School Performance." ADJC (1989): 1234-1239.

[3] T.A. Nicklas, et al. "Nutrient Adequacy of Low Fat Intakes for Children: The Bogalusa Heart Study." PEDIATRICS 89(2) (1992) 221-228.

[4] Ken Resnicow, "The Relationship Between Breakfast Habits and Plasma Cholesterol Levels in Schoolchildren." JOURNAL OF SCHOOL HEALTH 61(2) (1991): 81-85.

[5] Peggy Pipes, NUTRITION IN INFANCY AND CHILDHOOD. St Louis: Times Mirror/Mosby, 1985.

[6] Ellyn Satter, HOW TO GET YOUR KID TO EAT...BUT NOT TOO MUCH. Palo Alto: Bull Publishing, 1987.

[7] Satter.

The Breakfast Formula

Life, within doors, has few pleasanter prospects than a neatly arranged and well-provisioned breakfast table.

Nathaniel Hawthorne

The Breakfast Formula

The Breakfast Formula:
The Protein-Carbohydrate
Connection

Growl! Grumble!! Gurgle!!! Roar!!!! More than three hours remain until lunch, and those savage beasts in the stomach are at it again. Breakfast eaters may be thinking, "Why am I hungry so soon?" Skippers are probably too ravenous to ask why -- their minds are on the doughnuts sitting in the nearby office lounge!

At some point during the day, everybody has to deal with hunger. Some eat right away, while others allow the feeling to reach a certain threshold whereby only the most enticing (and probably fatty) foods satisfy! An interest in WHAT'S FOR BREAKFAST? indicates a realization that a change in eating habits is warranted. Change entails choice: one can either alter the reaction to hunger, or let hunger take control. This book illustrates how to plan a breakfast that will keep the stomach content well into the morning, via the Protein-Carbohydrate (alias Pro-Carb) Connection.

The Power of Protein

In the 1970's, a high protein diet was championed for everything from body building to hair restoration. Over-reliance on this or any other nutrient offers no guarantee these marvels will come to pass. Protein does aid in muscle tissue construction and repair, hair and fingernail growth, and hormone and red blood cell production. When necessary, protein energizes the muscles once carbohydrate runs out, such as during strict dieting, illness, or strenuous exercise. As with carbohydrate, excess protein calories are stored as body FAT.

Table 9: Complete Proteins (in 1-2 ounce serving sizes for breakfast)

Complete proteins provide all essential amino acids for cell growth and repair.

Lean red meat:	Extra lean ground beef; any round or loin cut; trimmed chuck roast, ham that is at least 95% lean by weight
Poultry:	Skinless chicken and turkey breast
Fish:	Water-packed tuna, all varieties of fresh or frozen unbattered fish
Eggs:	Limit egg yolks to 3-4 times weekly; use all the egg whites and egg substitutes desired (without added fat)
Milk or yogurt:	Nonfat or lowfat -- Skim, 1/2%, 1% -- 1 serving (8-10 fluid ounces)
Cheese:	Fat-free or low-fat -- 1-2 ounce servings or 1/2 cup servings of soft cheese, like cottage or farmer

Protein is composed of amino acids. The presence of all 12 essential amino acids in a protein molecule means it is *complete*. Meats, dairy products, and egg whites are complete.

When two incomplete proteins are combined they compliment one another, providing all essential amino acids.

Legumes, seeds, nuts and grains possess some, but not all, essential amino acids. These are classified as *incomplete*. Vegetarians must combine two of the "incomplete" proteins shown in Table 10 to have a "complete" package.   Combining two incomplete proteins furnishes all 12 essential amino acids. This is called protein complementation. Grains and legumes, legumes and nuts/seeds, and grains with nuts/seeds are trustworthy combinations. Contrary to past belief, it isn't necessary to complement protein foods at the same meal. Individuals can consume them separately throughout the course of the day[1,2].

Table 10: Incomplete Proteins

*Incomplete proteins do **not** have to be eaten at the same meal to compliment one another.*

Grains:	Wheat, corn, rice, barley (any of these can be eaten in the form of bread, cereal, or pasta)
Legumes:	Pinto beans, navy beans, red beans, kidney beans, lentils, black beans, black-eyed peas, tofu (soybean curd)
Nuts and seeds:	All types of nuts (eg. peanuts, walnuts, pecans, etc.) and seeds (sunflower, sesame, pumpkin, etc.). These work best as garnishes or accents to a meal,

How much protein is necessary? **A daily intake of 15-20% of total calories will do the job.** See Appendix D, page 251 on determining protein needs.

Carbohydrate Know-How

Are bread, potatoes, pasta, and rice "fattening"? Their bad reputation is undeserved because added fat is actually the guilty party. Bagels for instance, are quite low in fat (1 gram per bagel) until cream cheese is piled on top (at 5 grams per tablespoon)!

At least one out of every two calories should come from carbohydrate.

When food energy comes from carbohydrate, the body stores some of it as glycogen. Muscles count on glycogen to keep them going! Any leftover fuel the body doesn't need is packed away as body FAT.

Currently, Americans take in an average of 40-45% of their daily calories from carbohydrate. A preferable range is 50-60%, as the NCEP guidelines

Breakfast "Pro-Carb" Rule of Thumb: Strive for 15 g Protein and 40 g Carbohydrate at each morning meal.

suggest. Finally, something to eat MORE of instead of LESS! In fact, up to 65-70% carbohydrate calories are recommended for very active people (exercising 5-7 times weekly at least 30 minutes per session). A minimum of 40 grams of carbohydrate at breakfast is recommended.

Table 11: Carbohydrate Foods

Food	Serving Size
Whole Grain Cereals and Breads	1/2 cup or 1 slice
Potatoes, Rice, and Pasta	1/2 cup or a medium potato
Dried Beans and Peas	
(pinto beans, black-eyed peas, chickpeas, etc.)	1/2 cup
Fruits and Vegetables	1 whole piece,
(fresh, canned, or frozen)	1/2 cup loose pieces
	or sauce
Lowfat Dairy Products	1 cup fluid milk or yogurt,
	1/2 cup cottage cheese,
	frozen desserts,
	1 ounce cheese

A Word About Fruits and Vegetables

Fruits and vegetables lend a variety of flavors and nutritional benefits. Furthermore, their colors and textures are pleasing counterpoints to breads, cereals, and other grain products. Far too often, fruits and vegetables are the missing pieces in a sound breakfast.

If foods were appraised on the basis of color alone, fruits and veggies would win hands down! Note the lackluster hue and predictable flavor of doughnuts and croissants and the like. They have a "velvet curtain" quality, as master chef Graham Kerr puts it--lacking dimension and complexity. Fruits and veggies are diverse, and come in a wealth of shapes, shades, sizes, and flavors. Be a little daring and partake of this natural bounty.

Strive for 5 servings of fruit and vegetables each day.

The American Cancer Society recommends 5 servings a day of fruits and/or vegetables. An achievable goal is 1-2 fruit or vegetable servings at breakfast daily[3]. A serving consists of the following:

* One medium sized fresh fruit (Choose these more frequently for Vitamin C content: oranges, grapefruit, 5-6 whole strawberries, and kiwifruit)

* 1/2 cup of canned fruit or 1/2 cup cooked vegetables

* 1/2 cup sliced fresh fruit

* 2 tablespoons dried fruit

Fruits and vegetables are important carbohydrates.

* 1 cup of raw vegetables

* 1/2 cup unsweetened 100% fruit juice

Stock the pantry with citrus fruits, green leafy and orange vegetables for their vitamins A and C. Oranges, grapefruit, spinach, and carrots are a good start. The first two sound like typical breakfast items, and the others can be snuck into the meal without even noticing. Fresh spinach leaves accompany the MORNING BLT quite nicely (see page 159). Carrot sticks make an attractive garnish with any breakfast main dish.

What About Table Sugar?

Table sugar and honey supply copious calories but scant nutrients. It is suspected that inordinate amounts cause obesity, but scientific studies to date have demonstrated a direct link to tooth decay only. Obesity results from excessive calories of all foods (especially fat), and is a risk factor for heart disease and diabetes.

These sugars need not be banished, only moderated. To cut back, be on the lookout for jams, jellies, syrup, sweetened fruit drinks, and many sweetened children's cereals. Here are some suggestions for breakfast and other meals.

Suggestions to Reduce Added Sugar:

Tips and Hints to reduce added sugar.

*   Use fruit or artificial sweeteners on cereals or in beverages.

*   Substitute sugar-free jams and jellies for the regular versions.

*   Purchase canned fruits packed in water or in their own juices.

*   Instead of prepared fruit yogurt (one regular 8-oz container has the equivalent of 7 teaspoons of sugar!), mix fresh fruit with plain nonfat or lowfat yogurt.

*   It is a common belief that honey is healthier than sugar. Truth is, honey is not more nutritious--it is still sugar, only in a concentrated form.

*   Low-calorie maple and fruit syrups have 33-50% fewer calories than their analogues. Make a beeline toward these light brands, like Aunt Jemima Light®, Food Club Light®, Hungry Jack Light®, Log Cabin Light®, Mrs. Butterworth Light®, and Knotts Light®. However, it

may not be worth the effort to purchase them if a person ends up eating twice the amount.

* People who enjoy soda pop in the morning should keep in mind that one soft drink has up to 10 teaspoons of sugar a can! Choose diet drinks whenever possible.

What Makes You Hungry

A drop in blood sugar is one of several physiological cues indicating it's time to think about eating. After a person has been awake awhile (without food), blood sugar levels start to fall because it has likely been 8-12 hours since the last meal. What is eaten will greatly affect how long satisfaction persists. The question is, which foods will keep the appetite at bay until lunchtime?

The answer is a morning meal that combines both protein and carbohydrate (with a little fat to keep things tasty). This is inextricably linked to a series of events revolving around blood sugar (or blood glucose), and insulin.

When blood sugar levels fall, hunger increases.

When carbohydrate enters the intestine, it is broken down into its simplest form, glucose (also known as blood sugar). Next, the glucose is absorbed into the bloodstream from the intestine. For simplicity's sake, once glucose enters the bloodstream, we will refer to it as *blood sugar*. The body sends a signal for insulin to be released so blood sugar can be carried to the tissues. Blood sugar is then either utilized as an immediate fuel source or, is stored as glycogen (the stored form of carbohydrate) or fat.

A meal composed solely of carbohydrate (especially simple sugar) may cause glucose to "spill" into the bloodstream (from the intestines) too quickly. This triggers more insulin to be produced than is needed. The excessive release of insulin lowers your blood sugar to a level that further accelerates your appetite. This is why after eating a glazed doughnut for breakfast (high in sugar), hunger usually follows a short time later.

Protein combined with carbohydrate helps regulate blood sugar and insulin activity.

When protein is combined with carbohydrate in a meal, it slows down the passage of glucose into the bloodstream. A smidgen of fat (in line with daily goals--see Appendix F, page 252) slows it down even more. This means insulin levels are less likely to rise sharply, so blood sugar is less likely to plummet. The rewards for uniting these nutrients are satiety for longer periods and more power over when to eat and what is eaten[4]. Thus, a Pro-Carb connection is made!! See Table 12 (below) for a visual interpretation of the process.

Table 12: Effects of Carbohydrate and Carbohydrate/Protein on Blood Sugar Levels

Carbohydrate	Carbohydrate + Protein
Fast Conversion	Slower Conversion
Glucose	Glucose
Rapid Uptake	Slower Uptake
Blood Sugar	Blood Sugar
Strong Insulin Rush	Less insulin kicks in
Hunger within 2 hours	Fullness for 3-4 hours

Protein and carbohydrate eaten together prevent excess insulin activity.

Should the scenario described be difficult to follow, remember that carbohydrate accompanied by protein can prevent excess insulin activity. Too much insulin inevitably leads to a drop in blood sugar and an exorbitant increase in appetite before the next meal rolls around.

Nutrition Nugget

BEWARE! Breakfast skippers can develop a resistance to insulin.

Those not eating breakfast regularly, beware! Breakfast skippers can develop a resistance to the actions of insulin. When blood sugar can't get to needy tissues, the body responds by producing an overabundance of insulin. This causes more blood sugar to rush into the tissues than is needed at that particular time. The surplus blood sugar is more likely to be converted to fat. In the final analysis, frequent skipping of breakfast or any other meal is a no-win situation.

Being famished 1-2 hours after eating means something is missing from the meal. An effective pro-carb connection keeps you satisfied a good 3-4 hours. After this time elapses, it is natural to feel hungry again. Early risers who fill their stomachs before dawn need not feel guilty if they are foraging for sustenance by midmorning. These folks can pro-carb connect if they choose to have a midmorning snack.

Skipping breakfast is a no-win situation.

IMPORTANT NOTE:

Diminish the urge to splurge
with at least 15 grams of protein
and 40 grams of carbohydrate in the morning.
For midmorning snack purposes, consume foods
with at least 7 grams protein and 15 grams carbohydrate.

Note: The carbohydrate value of 40 grams is derived from the ideal breakfast plan of at least 1 fruit serving, 1 bread serving and 1 dairy serving. The protein value is derived from consuming either 2 dairy servings or 1 lean protein and 1 dairy serving. For the snack, the carbohydrate value comes from consuming 1 fruit, 1 bread or 1 dairy serving. The protein value comes from consuming 1 lean protein or 1 dairy serving.

When deciding to eat 1-2 ounces of meat at breakfast, keep in mind it only leaves 4-5 ounces of meat for the rest of the day. Balance intake accordingly. A suggestion is to skip meat altogether at lunch and have a 4-5 ounce portion at dinner or vice versa.

In order to hit these targets, variety is the key. A serving or two from each of these four food groups (fruit/vegetable, bread, cereal, and dairy) should have a standing reservation at your breakfast table. Meat can have an occasional guest spot when more protein is desired. Fats like oil and margarine can attend, but don't let them dominate the gathering. For practical use, this information translates into the Breakfast Formula.

THE BREAKFAST FORMULA:

1-2 servings of Whole Grain Bread or Cereal
1-2 servings of Fruits or Vegetables
1-2 servings of a low-fat Dairy product OR
1 serving (1-2 ounces) lean Protein
1 teaspoon Fat (optional)

"Pro-Carb"
Menus

The following menus connect protein and carbohydrate with just enough fat. They provide not only abundant energy, but also key nutrients like calcium, iron, and vitamins A and C. When noted, accompany each meal with an 8 fluid ounce glass of skim milk or nonfat yogurt, because either one adds another 8-10 grams of protein, 12 grams carbohydrate, and only 80 fat-free calories. When juice is specified as part of the menu, a small glass is 6 fluid ounces, while a large glass is 8 fluid ounces.

Menu 1: 1 cup chilled, ripe cantaloupe chunks, 1 Pillsbury brand biscuit (NOT "grand" or "country style") spread with 2 tablespoons PEANUT BUTTER CREAM (page 106). Serve with a glass of ice cold skim milk.

47 g Carbohydrate, 16 g Protein, 8 g Fat, 317 Calories.

"Pro-Carb"
Menus

Menu 2: 2 tablespoons light cream cheese, 1 thin slice lean ham (1 ounce) on a toasted whole grain bagel, fresh peach, and 8 ounces skim milk.

60 g Carbohydrate, 23 g Protein, 8 g Fat, 402 Calories.

Menu 3: 1 ounce reduced fat swiss cheese cubes, 6 whole wheat saltines, a piece of fresh fruit, and a glass of skim milk.

40 g Carbohydrate, 18 g Protein, 8 g Fat, 293 Calories.

Menu 4: One slice of lean ham (1 ounce), 1 ounce dried fruit (like apricots, apples, or dates), French roll, and 8 ounces skim milk.

63 g Carbohydrate, 21 g Protein, 5 g Fat, 376 Calories.

Note: Sodium-conscious individuals should select low-sodium ham and low-sodium cheese instead of the regular versions.

Menu 5: 1 French roll spread with 1 ounce Laughing Cow® reduced fat cheese, and topped with 1 tablespoon fruit preserves. Serve with a fresh apple and 8 ounces skim milk.

76 g Carbohydrate, 22 g Protein, 6 g Fat, 440 Calories.

Menu 6: Cinnamon raisin bagel spread with a mixture of 1/2 cup light ricotta cheese, 1 teaspoon sugar, and 1 sliced apple, served with milk.

75 g Carbohydrate, 29 g Protein, 12 g Fat, 516 Calories.

Menu 7: A medium baked potato (with skin) topped with 1 ounce light cheddar cheese, served with 8 ounces orange juice and 8 ounces lowfat chocolate milk.

97 g Carbohydrate, 21 g Protein, 10 g Fat, 554 Calories.

Menu 8: 2 ounces cold skinless chicken breast, corn tortilla (try blue corn for extra color!), lettuce, tomato, fat-free mayonnaise, lowfat chocolate milk, and a banana.

74 g Carbohydrate, 31 g Protein, 9 g Fat, 485 Calories.

Menu 9: 1/4 cup of leftover chicken, turkey, or tuna salad in a 1/2 pita

"Pro-Carb"
Menus continued

pocket, with lettuce leaf and 2 tomato slices. Garnish the plate with 4-5 fresh strawberries. Serve with a cup of skim milk.

40 g Carbohydrate, 18 g Protein, 9 g Fat, 314 Calories.

Menu 10: Hard boiled egg eaten with two pieces of whole wheat toast spread with 2 teaspoons jelly. Serve with a kiwi fruit and a glass of skim milk on the side.

57 g Carbohydrate, 22 g Protein, 9 g Fat, 377 Calories.

Menu 11: Fill a 1/2 pita with 2 1/8-ounce light deviled ham (1/2 small can), 1/3 cup canned unsweetened pineapple, and 2 teaspoons of chopped green onion. Wash it all down with skim milk and orange juice.

55 g Carbohydrate, 23 g Protein, 9 g Fat, 409 Calories.

Menu 12: Your favorite low-fat muffin with a serving of CINNAMON RICOTTA SPREAD (page 100), with an apple and nonfat yogurt on the side.

71 g Carbohydrate, 16 g Protein, 5 g Fat, 396 Calories.

Menu 13: Peanut butter, banana, and jelly waffle: Spread a toasted waffle with 1 tablespoon peanut butter and 2 teaspoons sugar-free jam or jelly. Top with 1/2 sliced banana. Accompany with 1/2 cup honeydew melon chunks and skim milk.

58 g Carbohydrate, 16 g Protein, 12 g Fat, 377 Calories.

Menu 14: Mix together 1/4 cup shredded fat-free cheddar cheese and 4 teaspoons fat-free cream cheese. Spread on two toasted bagel halves or 10 fat-free or low fat crackers. Top with 1 tablespoon regular or sugar-free fruit preserves. With 1 cup orange juice, this connection has

74 g Carbohydrate, 20 g Protein, 2 g Fat, 385 Calories.

Menu 15: Hard boiled egg, served with a PUMPKIN MUFFIN (see page

"Pro-Carb"
Menus continued

144 for recipe) spread with 1 tablespoon light cream cheese. Add segments from one large orange, and milk of course.

55 g Carbohydrate, 21 g Protein, 11 g Fat, 402 Calories.

"Morning Reuben": 1 ounce turkey pastrami on a rye bagel topped with 1 ounce fat-free or light cream cheese and 3 fresh unpeeled ripe pear slices, mustard or fat-free Thousand Island dressing. 8 ounces of 1% lowfat chocolate milk tastes especially good with this!

67 g Carbohydrate, 24 g Protein, 12 g Fat, 475 Calories.

"Bagel/Cheese Melt": Place one ounce light cheddar cheese on a garlic bagel, and broil until cheese melts. Serve with 2 tomato slices, an 8 ounce glass of low salt V-8® juice and a cup of skim milk.

67 g Carbohydrate, 21 g Protein, 6 g Fat, 451 Calories.

"Southern Traditions": Prepare 1 serving instant grits according to package directions. Add 2 ounces heated leftover turkey breast and 2 tablespoons low fat bottled gravy (such as Pepperidge Farms®). Serve with 2 tomato slices, 3-4 carrot sticks, and an 8 ounce glass of orange juice.

56 g Carbohydrate, 24 g Protein, 3 g Fat, 346 Calories.

"Quick Peanut Butter Crepes": 2 frozen pancakes rolled with 2 tablespoons PEANUT BUTTER CREAM (page 106). Warm in the microwave 30 seconds, and top with 1/2 cup chopped fresh fruit (kiwi or peaches), and a dusting of powdered sugar. Serve with lowfat chocolate milk.

80 g Carbohydrate, 17 g Protein, 11 g Fat, 481 Calories.

"Nacho Toast": Top 1 slice of toasted whole wheat bread with 3 tablespoons warm mashed pinto beans (or black-eyed peas). Sprinkle 1 tablespoon shredded light cheddar cheese and broil for 2-3 minutes. Garnish with lettuce, chopped tomato, and salsa. Eat with an orange and skim milk.

52 g Carbohydrate, 17 g Protein, 3 g Fat, 300 Calories.

"Pro-Carb" Rule: At least 15 g Protein and 40 g Carbohydrate at breakfast

"The Marie Elena Sandwich": (pro-carbing with a Cuban flair): Take a 6-inch long piece of French bread sliced lengthwise. On half, spread 1 tablespoon fat-free cream cheese, 2 teaspoons sugar-free strawberry preserves, and 1 ounce of lean ham or skinless chicken breast. Place other bread half on top and serve. Accompany with 1 sliced mango and skim milk.

77 g Carbohydrate, 23 g Protein, 10 g Fat, 459 Calories.

"Ham-Burger Deluxe": Take your favorite brand of hamburger bun and load it with one ounce of ham, one ounce of turkey, one slice fat-free American cheese, lettuce, 1 slice tomato, and a couple of pickle slices. Garnish with fat-free mayo, ketchup, or mustard. With a handful of grapes, this meal sends you off to greet the day in grand fashion.

40 g Carbohydrate, 24 g Protein, 6 g Fat, 330 Calories.

"Biscuit Sandwich": 1 medium biscuit (with no more than 3 grams fat) 1 ounce warm lean ham, and 1 egg, cooked any style (preferably without added fat). Top it off with 1/2 cup grapefruit segments and 8 ounces of chocolate skim milk.

56 g Carbohydrate, 23 g Protein, 10 g Fat, 430 Calories.

"Fair Dinkum Tucker" (means really great food in Australia): Toast an Oroweat brand Australian Cornbread Toaster Biscuit (or one of our biscuits on page 147+). Put a one ounce piece of cooked turkey sausage in between the halves and go to town! Add 8 oz. skim milk, and a nice juicy pear.

53 g Carbohydrate, 18 g Protein, 8 g Fat, 300 Calories.

"Apple Cream Cheese Pastry": Spread 1 tablespoon fat-free cream cheese on a toasted waffle. Top with 1/2 cup cinnamon applesauce and 1 tablespoon chopped walnuts. Wonderful with 3-4 cantaloupe wedges and skim milk.

68 g Carbohydrate, 16 g Protein, 8 g Fat, 411 Calories.

"Pro-Carb"
Menus continued

"Cocoa Cheese Muffin": Mix 2 tablespoons low-fat ricotta cheese with 1 1/2 teaspoons cocoa powder and 1 teaspoon sugar (or equivalent sugar substitute). Spread between two low-fat muffin halves (bran or banana work very well). Peach slices and skim milk complete this menu.

51 g Carbohydrate, 15 g Protein, 4 g Fat, 289 Calories.

"Spanish Omelet": 1/2 cup egg substitute, cooked, stuffed into two pita bread halves along with 1/2 cup tomato slices and a tablespoon of picante salsa. Serve with slices from a mango or papaya.

64 g Carbohydrate, 16 g Protein, 2 g Fat, 320 Calories.

"Quick Breakfast Lasagna": Combine 1 cup leftover cooked pasta, 4 tablespoons spaghetti sauce, 1/2 cup lowfat cottage cheese, 2 tablespoons grated part skim mozzarella cheese, and 1 teaspoon Parmesan cheese. Microwave for 1 minute on high

48 g Carbohydrate, 26 g Protein, 5 grams Fat, 353 Calories.

"Skinny Pig-in-a-Blanket": Wrap a lean hot dog (less than 3 grams fat per wiener) with 1 small canned biscuit and bake for 10 minutes at 350° F. Serve with 1/2 cup seedless green grapes and 1 cup chocolate skim milk.

54 g Carbohydrate, 18 g Protein, 5 g Fat, 339 Calories.

"Chicken Cheese Toast": Two toasted English muffin halves each topped with 1/4 cup chopped cooked chicken, 1 tomato slice, and a half ounce of light Monterey Jack cheese. Broil until cheese melts. Serve with an apple.

50 g Carbohydrate, 23 g Protein, 8 g Fat, 358 Calories.

"Catch of the Day": Flake a leftover piece of cooked whitefish (2 ounces) and mix with a combination of 1 tablespoon fat-free mayonnaise and 1 tablespoon light salad dressing (French or Italian). Serve with 9 fat-free crackers and a large pear.

44 g Carbohydrate, 19 g Protein, 1 g Fat, 305 Calories.

"Pro-Carb"
Menus continued

"Speedy Shrimp Toast": Place 1 ounce of cooked shrimp (chopped) and 1 ounce shredded light cheddar cheese on a piece of whole grain toast. Place under broiler until cheese melts. Serve with 2 mineolas (a type of tangelo) and skim milk.

47 g Carbohydrate, 27 g Protein, 8 g Fat, 370 Calories.

"Popcorn Cereal": Surely, we jest! Seriously, LM Boyd of the Informed Source revealed that this concoction was savored by many an early American colonist. For the modernized version, prepare 4 popped cups of light microwave popcorn, unbuttered. Let cool slightly. Place in large bowl and add 3/4 cup lowfat milk, 1/4 cup evaporated skim milk, 1 tbsp honey, and 1/2 banana, sliced. Serve with a small glass of orange juice.

85 g Carbohydrate, 20 g Protein, 6 g Fat, 458 Calories.

"Tummy Warmer": Mix 1 ounce leftover chopped cooked chicken breast into 1 cup of reduced fat cream soup (diluted with skim milk). Serve hot with 10 saltine crackers, and a small glass of orange juice.

56 g Carbohydrate, 19 g Protein, 6 g Fat, 358 Calories.

"Good Morning Chicken and Rice": Mix 1 cup leftover cooked rice with 2 ounces leftover cooked chopped chicken breast and 1 ounce light cheddar cheese. Microwave on high until warm, about 1-2 minutes. Serve with a small French roll and 6 fluid ounces low salt vegetable juice (eg. V-8).

63 g Carbohydrate, 27 g Protein, 9 g Fat, 455 Calories.

"Tortilla Cheese Roll-ups": Place 2 corn tortillas on microwave safe plate. Sprinkle each tortilla with 1 ounce shredded light Monterey Jack cheese. Microwave until cheese melts. Add a teaspoon of low-sodium PICANTE SAUCE (page 190) to each. Roll up and serve with 1 cup fresh pineapple chunks and 1 cup of MEXICAN HOT CHOCOLATE (page 180).

74 g Carbohydrate, 31 g Protein, 14 g Fat, 563 Calories.

"Pro-Carb"
Menus continued

"Breakfast Sub": Stuff a whole wheat submarine bun with 1 ounce lean sliced ham, 1 ounce sliced turkey breast, 1 ounce light Swiss cheese (with 2 grams fat per serving), lettuce leaf, and 2 tomato slices. Accompany the sandwich with 8 fluid ounces of your favorite juice.

101 g Carbohydrate, 34 g Protein, 11 g Fat, 654 Calories.

"Western Scramble": In a heated 10-inch skillet that has been coated with vegetable cooking spray, combine 1/2 cup egg substitute, 2 ounces leftover cooked chopped potato, 1 tablespoon green onion, 2 teaspoons green pepper, and 1 slice cooked turkey bacon, crumbled. Cook until eggs are set and vegetables are tender. Serve with 6 ounces cranberry juice and a slice of toast spread with 2 teaspoons sugar-free preserves.

53 g Carbohydrate, 15 g Protein, 4 g Fat, 304 Calories.

"Stuffed Potato": A medium leftover baked potato stuffed with 2 ounces chopped cooked lean beef and 1 ounce shredded light cheddar cheese (choose one with no more than 3 grams fat per ounce). Microwave on high until cheese melts (about 1-2 minutes).

77 g Carbohydrate, 17 g Protein, 6 g Fat, 440 Calories.

"Breakfast Taco": Mix together 1 ounce of cooked crumbled COUN-TRY SAUSAGE (see page 185), 1/4 cup OVEN FRIED POTATOES (page 202), and 1/2 cup scrambled egg substitute (cooked without fat). Place mixture on a warm 8-inch flour tortilla, roll, then serve.

53 grams Carbohydrate, 24 g Protein, 7 g Fat, 380 Calories.

CALCI-OATMEAL: In a small microwave-safe bowl, mix one package instant oatmeal with 5 fluid ounces evaporated skim milk. Microwave 1-2 minutes on high. Add 1/2 cup fresh or canned unsweetened peaches, chopped. Delicious, with 568 milligrams calcium per serving!

52 g Carbohydrate, 18 g Protein, 2 g Fat, 300 Calories.

"Pro-Carb"
Rule: At least 15
g Protein and 40
g Carbohydrate
at breakfast

Try using one or more of our delicious recipes to create your own connection, such as:

BLUEBERRY BANANA SHAKE (see page 91) and a toasted English muffin spread with 2 tablespoons fat-free cream cheese.

83 g Carbohydrate, 19 g Protein, 5 g Fat, 434 Calories.

PEACH SMOOTHIE (see page 92) and a small (6-inch) flour tortilla rolled up with 1 ounce of lean, cooked beef strips.

41 g Carbohydrate, 15 g Protein, 5 g Fat, 280 Calories.

MANGO BANANA FRAPPE (see page 94) with a toasted honey-raisin bagel spread with 2 teaspoons sugar-free preserves.

83 g Carbohydrate, 16 g Protein, 3 g Fat, 410 Calories.

FRUIT PIZZA (see page 113) and CAPPUCCINO FREEZE (see page 95)

86 g Carbohydrate, 21 g Protein, 13 g Fat, 560 Calories.

SHRIMP TACO (see page 120) supplemented with 1/4 cup mashed pinto beans, a cup of lowfat milk and your choice of fresh fruit.

51 g Carbohydrate, 26 g Protein, 7 g Fat, 364 Calories.

MEGA MUFFIN (see page 122) with an 8-ounce glass of fruit juice.

69 g Carbohydrate, 23 g Protein, 8 g Fat, 398 Calories.

PAN FRIED FRENCH TOAST (see page 112) with a glass of grapefruit juice.

79 g Carbohydrate, 17 g Protein, 11 g Fat, 497 Calories.

PEACH SMOOTHIE (see page 92) and a WAFFLE SANDWICH (see page 119).

65 g Carbohydrate, 14 g Protein, 9 g Fat, 380 Calories.

Menus using
WHAT'S FOR
BREAKFAST
recipes

Transcontinental: SWISS OATMEAL (see page 197) and MEXICAN HOT COCOA (see page 180).

60 g Carbohydrate, 17 g Protein, 6 g Fat, 360 Calories.

SOFT TACO WITH BACON, EGG AND CORN (see page 124) and a small glass of juice.

44 g Carbohydrate, 15 g Protein, 9 g Fat, 318 Calories.

CHEESY GRITS CASSEROLE (see page 173) served with a toasted English muffin, fresh apple, and a glass of chocolate skim milk.

58 g Carbohydrate, 15 g Protein, 5 g Fat, 360 Calories.

"ORZO IT SEEMS" CEREAL (see page 117) with a 12 ounce glass of skim milk.

76 g Carbohydrate, 16 g Protein, 7 g Fat, 440 Calories

OAT BRAN WITH PEACH BUTTER (see page 118) accompanied by a slice of cinnamon raisin toast spread with a teaspoon of light tub margarine. Add a glass of 1/2% milk and you're on your way!

69 g Carbohydrate, 15 g Protein, 5 g Fat, 410 Calories.

2 BROCCOLI AND CHEESE MUFFINS (see page 146) and an 8 ounce cup of plain or fruited lowfat yogurt.

51 g Carbohydrate, 21 g Protein, 6 g Fat, 366 Calories.

2 TURKEY SAUSAGE AND CHEESE BISCUITS (see page 149) and a glass of lowfat buttermilk or skim milk.

46 g Carbohydrate, 18 g Protein, 10 g Fat, 360 Calories.

One warm slice of LIGHT CORNBREAD (see page 150) which has 12 fluid ounces warm skim milk poured on top. Serve topped with 1 tablespoon maple syrup. On the side, serve a 1/2 cup of sliced bananas and

"Pro-Carb"
recipes continued

fresh strawberries.

> *68 g Carbohydrate, 18 g Protein, 4 g Fat, 400 Calories.*

EGG STUFFED POTATO (see page 163) with a 6-ounce glass of grape juice.

> *49 g Carbohydrate, 15 g Protein, 3 g Fat, 300 Calories.*

EGG AND CHORIZO IN POTATO SKIN (see page 164) all by itself!

> *54 g Carbohydrate, 23 g Protein, 8 g Fat, 373 Calories.*

CHEESE POTATO OMELET (see page 166) with a slice of toast and a 6-ounce glass of juice.

> *50 g Carbohydrate, 24 g Protein, 7 g Fat, 360 Calories.*

Brown Bag a leftover HAM AND CHEESE CALZONE WITH APPLES (see page 206) that has been warmed in a microwave oven on medium for 1-1 1/2 minutes.

> *47 g Carbohydrate, 20 g Protein, 9 g Fat, 368 Calories.*

A serving of leftover CASSEROLE DE LA CASA(see page 169) with a glass of skim milk is a real morning eye-opener.

> *46 g Carbohydrate, 25 g Protein, 10 g Fat, 370 Calories.*

A slice of CANADIAN BACON BREAD (see page 162) with a cup of lowfat yogurt and a fresh pear fills you up the right way.

> *40 g Carbohydrate, 20 g Protein, 6 g Fat, 315 Calories.*

A leftover slice of SEAFOOD QUICHE (see page 212), slices from one medium apple, and a small glass of juice.

> *41 g Carbohydrate, 24 g Protein, 12 g Fat, 403 Calories.*

"Pro-Carb"
recipes continued

Notice how these meals combine foods from several groups (eg. milk and dairy, bread and cereal, fruit, vegetable, and meat). Substitutions can be made within each food group as desired to keep the nutrient balance in check. For instance, an apple or orange instead of a pear is fine. On the other hand, ham won't substitute for a bagel because it is from a different group. Similarly, cereal is not a substitute for an egg.

Experiment with the many different pro-carb connection menus, as one may work better than another.

Nutrition Note: It seems there are many diet fads that tout a high protein, low carbohydrate diet for hunger and weight control. The pro-carb connection concept differs in that it doesn't restrict carbohydrate intake. In fact, 50-60% of total calories in a meal should preferably be from carbohydrate, 15-20% from protein, and 30% or less from fat.

Recipe Introduction

This book favors easy-to-prepare breakfasts.

Breakfast can be the most monotonous of meals. Certainly, creativity and initiative are ordinarily at their lowest points when stumbling out of bed. But we don't have to revert to the same old standbys every morning. With a little assistance from WHAT'S FOR BREAKFAST? the first meal of the day can be the best of them all.

Besides optimal taste and nutritional value, this book favors easy to prepare breakfasts. Most of the recipes epitomize quick and simple "Monday through Friday" fare, utilizing everyday ingredients. Traditional favorites, modified to reduce the fat content, are included with less conventional but equally scrumptious dishes.

In today's world, people's lives are hurried and hectic. Consequently, the recipes are arranged according to cooking time. The many recipes in the "Do Ahead" category can be assembled today for rapid service tomorrow. This category also includes several dishes well suited for special occasions that require less than 1 hour preparation time. The "Super Quick" (less than 15 minutes) and "Quick" (15 to 35 minutes) sections consist of recipes suited to every situation, from a Sunday brunch to a Monday morning meeting.

Each recipe is analyzed for nutrient and diet exchanges.

Each recipe has been analyzed with the Nutritionist III and IV DINE software program (N-Squared Computing, 3040 Commercial St. SE, Suite 240, Salem OR 97302). Values are provided for calories, fat (in grams--g), protein (g), carbohydrate (g), sodium (in milligrams--mg), cholesterol (mg), saturated fat (g), and diet exchanges.

All values have been rounded to the next highest figure if they are over one-half of the unit of measurement.

Recipe Preparation

Cooking utensils and types of ingredients are important to consider.

Cooking Utensils: A fundamental tool for reducing fat content is the nonstick skillet. Many dishes can be cooked without liquid oils, relying instead on vegetable cooking spray. Also, when vegetable cooking spray is part of the recipe ingredients, it means one 3-second spray. If more than one spray is necessary, the number of recommended sprays is noted and included in the nutritional analysis. It's OK to try less if it prevents sticking.

Oil and Margarine: In recipes which call for fat, either an acceptable oil or margarine was used. The preferred oil was canola because of its low saturated fat content. Select margarines that are either light tub or regular stick, and made from a preferred oil such as corn, safflower, or canola (see page 229 for brand name suggestions).

Eggs and Egg Substitutes: Because of their lower fat and cholesterol content, egg whites or egg substitute (eg. Fleischmann's Egg Beaters®) replace whole eggs in many cases.

Rule of Thumb: Not all the foods eaten have to be 30% or less calories from fat! The cumulative total for a day or group of days should be aimed toward 30% or less.

Salt: Seasonings in virtually any recipe (excluding baked goods) can be adjusted to taste, including salt (see page 237 for a list of seasoning suggestions for a variety of breakfast foods).

Recipe Categories

"Super Quick" breakfasts can entice breakfast rookies, as they take 15 minutes or less. Children are more likely to eat what they have helped to prepare, so try to get them involved with making recipes in this category.

The "Quick" recipes require an average of 15-35 minutes preparation time, good for the average workday or a busy weekend.

Many "Do Ahead" recipes can be made in advance and are utilized in "Super Quick" and "Quick" recipes where designated. Other recipes in the "Make Ahead" section should be reserved for those times when 35 minutes or longer can be devoted to an exceptional meal.

Notes

[1] Gary Null, THE VEGETARIAN HANDBOOK. New York: St. Martin's Press, 1987.

[2] American Dietetic Association. Position of the American Dietetic Association: Vegetarian Diets--Technical Support Paper. JOURNAL OF THE AMERICAN DIETETIC ASSOCIATION. 88 (1988) 352-355.

[3] U.S. Department of Health and Human Services. EAT MORE FRUITS AND VEGETABLES: 5 A DAY FOR BETTER HEALTH. Washington: 1991.

[4] Marie V. Krause, and Mahan, L. Kathleen. FOOD, NUTRITION, AND DIET THERAPY. Philadelphia: W.B. Sanders, 1992.

Super Quick Recipes

*As more people entered the workforce,
the pace of life accelerated to the point
that skipping breakfast became
an all-too-common practice.*

Donna Roy

Super Quick Recipes

BLUEBERRY BANANA SHAKE

Blueberries and bananas are a great flavor combination while the buttermilk gives a tartness similar to yogurt. Because blueberries (like most berries) are high in fiber, this shake provides 4 grams in one serving.

Serves 1

1/2	cup frozen blueberries
1	medium banana, frozen (or 1 fresh banana and 2 ice cubes)
1	cup lowfat buttermilk
4	teaspoons sugar (or equivalent sugar substitute)

Combine all ingredients in blender and process until smooth, about 15-30 seconds.

Nutrient Analysis: 1 serving
304 Calories, 3 g Fat, 10 g Protein, 57 g Carbohydrate, 4 g Fiber, 258 mg Sodium, 9 mg Cholesterol,
1 g Sat Fat.
Exchanges: 1 milk, 3 1/2 fruit.

Breakfast is a forecast of the whole day;
spoil that, and all is spoiled.

Leigh Hunt

PEACH SMOOTHIE

Be sure to enjoy this quick breakfast beverage when fresh peaches are in season.
It's featured on the cover of this book!

Serves 1

3/4   cup skim milk
1   medium to large fresh peach, peeled and pitted
2   tablespoons sugar (or equivalent sugar substitute)
2 - 3 drops almond extract
4   ice cubes

Combine all ingredients in blender and process until smooth, about 15-30 seconds.

Nutrient Analysis: 1 serving
191 Calories, 0 g Fat, 7 g Protein, 40 g Carbohydrate, 95 mg Sodium, 4 mg Cholesterol,
0 g Sat Fat.
Exchanges: 1 milk, 2 fruit

STRAWBERRY YOGURT SHAKE

Don't have time to sit down to eat breakfast? Whip this up in the blender and drink while getting dressed.

Serves 1

8   **frozen strawberries**
3/4   **cup plain nonfat yogurt**
1/4   **cup skim milk**
3   **ice cubes**
4   **teaspoons sugar (or equivalent sugar substitute)**

Process all ingredients in blender until smooth, about 30-45 seconds.

Nutrient Analysis: 1 serving
297 Calories, 1 g Fat, 13 g Protein, 64 g Carbohydrate, 3 g Fiber, 167 mg Sodium, 5 mg Cholesterol,
0 g Sat Fat.
Exchanges: 1 milk, 3 fruit

STRAWBERRY BANANA BREEZE

Serves 1

8   **frozen strawberries**
1   **medium banana**
1/4   **cup plus 2 tablespoons apple juice**

Place all ingredients in blender for 1 minute. Serve immediately.

Nutrient Analysis: 1 serving
243 Calories, 0 g Fat, 1 g Protein, 58 g Carbohydrate, 11 mg Sodium, 0 mg Cholesterol,
0 g Sat Fat.
Exchanges: 4 fruit.

CRAN-RASPBERRY COOLER

Serves 1

1/3   cup lowfat vanilla yogurt
1/3   cup frozen cran-raspberry juice concentrate
1/3   cup egg substitute, thawed

Mix all ingredients in blender or food processor until well-combined, about 15-20 seconds. Pour into chilled glass.

Nutrient Analysis: 1 serving
263 Calories, 1 g Fat, 11 g Protein, 52 g Carbohydrate, 179 mg Sodium, 4 mg Cholesterol,
0 g Sat Fat.
Exchanges: 1 milk, 3 fruit.

MANGO BANANA FRAPPE

This powerhouse beverage is sweetened naturally with mango. If you protein-fortify the skim milk (page 16), you have an instant "pro-carb connection" all by itself!

Serves 1

1   whole ripe mango, peeled, cored, and sliced
1/2   medium banana
1   cup skim milk
5   ice cubes

Place all ingredients in blender container and blend until smooth, about 20-30 seconds.

Nutrient Analysis: 1 serving
274 Calories, 1 g Fat, 11 g Protein, 55 g Carbohydrate, 5 g Fiber, 131 mg Sodium, 5 mg Cholesterol,
0 g Sat Fat.
Exchanges: 1 milk, 3 fruit.

CAPPUCCINO FREEZE

Serves 1

1	cup ice milk (vanilla, coffee or cappucino flavored, no nuts)
1/4	cup prepared black coffee, cooled
2	ice cubes
1/2	teaspoon cinnamon
1	tablespoon non-dairy whipped topping (optional)

Place first four ingredients in blender or food processor and mix until well-blended, about 15-20 seconds. Top with 1 tablespoon light non-dairy whipped topping, if desired.

Nutrient Analysis: 1 serving (without whipped topping)
195 Calories, 6 g Fat, 6 g Protein, 29 g Carbohydrate, 108 mg Sodium, 18 mg Cholesterol,
3 g Sat Fat.
Exchanges: 1 milk, 1 fruit, 1 fat.

Variation: COCONUT CAPPUCINO FREEZE

**Omit cinnamon and add 1 teaspoon coconut extract.
Top with 2 teaspoons shredded coconut.**

BANANA BOAT

Rich, crunchy, and appealing to the eye.

Serves 1

1	large banana
1	tablespoon peanut butter
1	tablespoon Grape Nuts® cereal
1	tablespoon raisins
1	teaspoon mini chocolate chip morsels

With peel intact, split banana lengthwise along inside curve about three quarters deep into the banana. Open banana just enough so there is room for the fillings. Spread peanut butter inside the banana. Sprinkle next three ingredients on top of peanut butter. Place banana in microwave with the open side facing upward and microwave on high for 1 minute.

To serve: Using the peel as a bowl, eat right out of the banana with a spoon.

Nutrient Analysis: 1 banana boat
273 Calories, 9 g Fat, 6 g Protein, 42 g Carbohydrate, 128 mg Sodium, 0 mg Cholesterol,
2 g Sat Fat.
Exchanges: 3 fruit, 2 fat.

BREAKFAST BANANA SPLIT

Great for children's parties!

Serves 1 adult, 2 children

1/2   **banana, sliced**
1   **cup custard-style lowfat vanilla yogurt**
1/4   **cup crushed pineapple, drained**
1   **teaspoon non-dairy whipped topping**
1   **teaspoon chopped nuts**
Maraschino cherry for garnish

Place banana slices into bowl. Spoon yogurt and crushed pineapple on top. Garnish with whipped topping, nuts, and cherry.

Nutrient Analysis: 1 serving (adult size)
331 Calories, 5 g Fat, 14 g Protein, 56 g Carbohydrate, 186 mg Sodium, 27 mg Cholesterol,
1 g Sat Fat.
Exchanges: 1 milk, 3 fruit, 1 fat.

Tell me what you eat,
and I will tell you what you are.

Brillat-Savarin

YOGURT SUNDAES

Would your kids like a special breakfast treat on Saturday morning? Have at least four toppings available and allow your children to create masterpieces.

6 - 8 ounces lowfat vanilla yogurt

Topping Possibilities:

Banana slices   **Fresh or frozen blueberries**
Fresh or frozen strawberries   **Unsweetened crushed pineapple**
Honey, maple syrup or molasses   **Lowfat granola**
Graham crackers (squares or teddy bear shapes)   **Gingersnaps, crushed**
Mini waffles, toasted until crisp   **Peanut butter (1 - 1 1/2 tablespoons)**
Chopped, dried fruit (eg. raisins, dates, or apricots)
Crushed Newton® or Snack Well® cookies
Light non-dairy whipped topping as a garnish

In a see-through serving glass, cup, or bowl, alternate yogurt and toppings. Repeat process until you have at least 3 different layers.

Nutrient Analysis: 1 serving
252 Calories, 4 g Fat, 12 g Protein, 41 g Carbohydrate, 215 mg Sodium, 16 mg Cholesterol,
0 g Sat Fat.
Exchanges: 1 milk, 2 fruit, 1 fat.

The nutritional breakdown varies due to the number of ingredients and the many different combination possibilities. All toppings listed (except peanut butter) are low in fat. One example of a tasty topping combination is 3/4 cup lowfat yogurt, 1/4 cup sliced strawberries, two gingersnaps, two tablespoons unsweetened crushed pineapple, and 1/2 banana. Our nutrient analysis is based on this combination.

FRUIT FIESTA

This colorful dish is a storehouse of Vitamin A and C. Serve with the SHRIMP TORTILLA (page 120) and skim milk for a delightful "pro-carb" connection.

Serves 2

1/2	medium cantaloupe
2	kiwis, peeled and sliced
1	mango, peeled and sliced
1/2	cup sliced fresh strawberries

Scoop out cantaloupe, taking care to leave the shell intact. Cube the cantaloupe flesh and mix with the other fruits. Place mixed fruit in cantaloupe shell, and top with lowfat lemon yogurt if desired.

Nutrient Analysis: 1 serving (without lemon yogurt)
144 Calories, 1 g Fat, 3 g Protein, 33 g Carbohydrate, 6 g Fiber, 11 mg Sodium, 0 mg Cholesterol,
0 g Sat Fat.
Exchanges: 2 1/2 fruit.

APPLEBERRY SAUCE

A no-cook, no-fuss topper for pancakes, waffles, or French toast. Substitute sugar-free jam or preserves if desired.

3/4 cup; 6 servings

1/2   cup chunky unsweetened applesauce
1/4   cup berry preserves (strawberry, blueberry, or blackberry)
1 1/2 teaspoons lemon juice

Combine all ingredients until smooth. To serve warm, heat syrup in microwave safe container on high for 30 seconds.

Nutrient Analysis: 1 serving (2 tablespoons, using regular preserves):
62 Calories, 0 g Fat, 0 g Protein, 15 g Carbohydrate, 2 mg Sodium, 0 mg Cholesterol,
0 g Sat Fat.
Exchanges: 1 fruit.

CINNAMON RICOTTA SPREAD

1/4 cup; 4 servings

1/4   cup low-fat ricotta cheese
1   tablespoon sugar (or equivalent sugar substitute)
1   teaspoon cinnamon

Mix all ingredients together and serve.

Nutrient Analysis: 1 serving (1 tablespoon)
31 Calories, 1 g Fat, 2 g Protein, 4 g Carbohydrate, 16 mg Sodium, 5 mg Cholesterol,
1 g Sat Fat.
Exchanges: 1/2 fruit.

APPLESAUCE YOGURT TOPPING

Spoon over pancakes, waffles, even the potato ROSTI (page 165).

1 cup; 4 servings

1/2	cup unsweetened applesauce
1/2	cup nonfat plain yogurt
4	teaspoons sugar (or equivalent sugar substitute)

Mix all ingredients together and serve.

Nutrient Analysis: 1 serving (1/4 cup, made with sugar)
33 Calories, 0 g Fat, 2 g Protein, 7 g Carbohydrate, 20 mg Sodium, 1 mg Cholesterol,
0 g Sat Fat.
Exchanges: 1/2 fruit.

APRICOT ALMOND SPREAD

1/2 cup; 8 servings

1/2   cup sugar-free apricot fruit spread
2   tablespoons sliced almonds
1/2   teaspoon almond extract

Mix ingredients together and serve.

Nutrient Analysis: 1 serving (1 tablespoon)
61 Calories, 1 g Fat, o g Protein, 13 g Carbohydrate, 0 mg Sodium, 0 mg Cholesterol,
0 g Sat Fat.
Exchanges:1 fruit

BANANA PEANUT BUTTER

1/2 cup; 8 servings

1   medium ripe banana
2   tablespoons apple juice
1   tablespoon peanut butter

Mash banana well. Stir in apple juice and peanut butter, then serve immediately.

Nutrient Analysis: 1 serving (1 tablespoon)
27 Calories, 1 g Fat, 1 g Protein, 4 g Carbohydrate, 10 mg Sodium, 0 mg Cholesterol,
0 g Sat Fat.
Exchanges: 1/2 fruit.

BLUEBERRY LEMON SAUCE

Perfect for pancakes or waffles.

2 cups; 16 servings

1   package (12-ounces) frozen blueberries, thawed
3   tablespoons sugar (or equivalent sugar substitute)
1   tablespoon cornstarch
1/2   cup water
1   tablespoon lemon juice

Drain thawed blueberries. Set aside. Combine sugar and cornstarch in saucepan. Add water and stir until blended. Cook over medium heat until mixture boils, stirring constantly. Reduce heat; simmer 1 minute. Stir in lemon juice and blueberries. Remove from heat. Serve warm or cold.

Nutrient Analysis: 1 serving (2 tablespoons)
21 Calories, 0 g Fat, 0 g Protein, 5 g Carbohydrate, 0 mg Sodium, 0 mg Cholesterol,
0 g Sat. Fat.
Exchanges: Free.

CASHEW CREAM CHEESE

Cashews contain saturated fat, so we added just enough of them to give this recipe a subtle, yet nutty flavor.

1/2 cup; 8 servings

1/4   cup fat-free cream cheese, softened
2   tablespoons nonfat plain yogurt
2   teaspoons sugar (or equivalent sugar substitute)
4   teaspoons chopped cashews

Mix all ingredients together until well-blended.

Nutrient Analysis: 1 serving (1 tablespoon)
22 Calories, 1 g Fat, 2 g Protein, 2 g Carbohydrate, 43 mg Sodium, 1 mg Cholesterol,
0 g Sat Fat.
Exchanges: Free (for 1 tablespoon).

LEMON BREAKFAST CREAM

1 1/2 cups; 12 servings

1   cup lowfat lemon yogurt
4   ounces (1/2 cup) light cream cheese
1   tablespoon lemon juice

Drain lemon yogurt for 3-4 hours if a thicker consistency is desired. See page 187 for directions. Soften cream cheese in microwave for 15-30 seconds on high. Then mix remaining ingredients together and serve.

Nutrient Analysis: 1 serving (2 tablespoons)
40 Calories, 2 g Fat, 2 g Protein, 4 g Carbohydrate, 64 mg Sodium, 7 mg Cholesterol,
1 g Sat Fat.
Exchanges: 1 fat.

The concept of variety in your diet is priceless.
Variety means never having to say
you are deprived of nutrients.

The Authors

MANDARIN ORANGE TOPPING

Great on pancakes, waffles and French toast.

1/2 cup; 4 servings

1   can (11-ounces) mandarin orange segments, with syrup
1   teaspoon cornstarch
2   teaspoons frozen orange juice concentrate
2   teaspoons orange-flavored liqueur (Grand Marnier®, Cointreau®, Triple Sec)

Drain mandarin orange segments. Put drained oranges in small saucepan. Mash with fork against sides and bottom of pan until orange segments are broken into small pieces. Stir in cornstarch and frozen orange juice concentrate. Bring to a boil, then cook over medium heat 1-2 minutes or until thickened. Remove from heat; strain through a small sieve to remove any excess liquid. Add orange-flavored liqueur.

Nutrient Analysis: 1 serving (2 tablespoons)
60 Calories, 0 g Fat, 0 g Protein, 14 g Carbohydrate, 6 mg Sodium, 0 mg Cholesterol,
0 g Sat Fat.
Exchanges: 1 fruit.

PEANUT BUTTER CREAM

When added to a meal of two slices of toast and a glass of skim milk, the percentage of fat overall drops to 20%.

1 1/4 cups; 10 servings

1/2   **cup fat-free ricotta cheese**
1/2   **cup fat-free cream cheese**
1/4   **cup peanut butter**
2   **tablespoons sugar (or equivalent sugar substitute)**
2   **tablespoons skim milk**
1 1/2 **teaspoons real vanilla extract**

Place ingredients into a food processor fitted with a metal blade and process until smooth, about 10 seconds.

Nutrient Analysis: 1 serving (2 tablespoons)
71 Calories, 4 g Fat, 5 g Protein, 5 g Carbohydrate, 91 mg Sodium, 4 mg Cholesterol,
1 g Sat Fat.
Exchanges: 1 meat.

PEAR HONEY BUTTER

Delicious served with SOUR CREAM PANCAKES (page 153).

1 cup; 4 servings

1   **can (16-ounces) pear halves, packed in juice**
2   **tablespoons honey**

Drain pears; reserve juice for another use. Mash pears to the consistency of chunky applesauce, using a potato masher or pastry blender. Stir in honey. Serve warm or cold.

Nutrient Analysis: 1 serving (1/4 cup)
88 Calories, 0 g Fat, 0 g Protein, 22 g Carbohydrate, 4 mg Sodium, 0 mg Cholesterol,
0 g Sat Fat.
Exchanges: 1 1/2 fruit.

VANILLA MAPLE CREAM SYRUP

Serve atop pancakes or waffles. Use natural maple syrup to realize the full flavor potential of this cream.

1 cup; 8 servings

1/3   **cup light cream cheese**
1/3   **cup vanilla lowfat yogurt**
1/3 cup maple syrup (regular or low calorie)

Soften cream cheese in microwave for 10-20 seconds on high. Add yogurt and stir until well blended. Mix syrup in gradually until smooth.

Nutrient Analysis: 1 serving (2 tablespoons, using regular maple syrup in the recipe)
68 Calories, 2 g Fat, 2 g Protein, 10 g Carbohydrate, 46 mg Sodium, 6 mg Cholesterol,
1 g Sat Fat.
Exchanges: 1 fruit.

Sow an act and you reap a habit.
Sow a habit and you reap a character.
Sow a character and you reap a destiny.

Charles Reade

VANILLA SOUR CREAM

Marvelous with French toast or pancakes.

1/2 cup; 4 servings

1/2   **cup light sour cream**
3   **teaspoons powdered sugar**
1/4   **teaspoon vanilla extract**

Mix all ingredients together and serve.

Nutrient Analysis: 1 serving (2 tablespoons)
48 Calories, 2 g Fat, 2 g Protein, 4 g Carbohydrate, 20 mg Sodium, 6 mg Cholesterol,
1 g Sat Fat.
Exchanges: 1 fat.

Variation: HAWAIIAN SOUR CREAM

Add 2 tablespoons canned, drained, crushed unsweetened pineapple.

BANANA CINNAMON TOAST

The bananas, cinnamon, and brown sugar are reminiscent of Bananas Foster. "Pro-carb connect" by serving a glass of CRAN-RASPBERRY COOLER (page 94) on the side.

Serves 1

1/2   large banana
1   slice whole wheat bread, toasted
2   teaspoons light tub margarine, melted
1 1/2 teaspoons brown sugar (or equivalent sugar substitute)
1/8   teaspoon cinnamon

Slice banana half into 4 slices lengthwise and place on toast. Drizzle melted margarine over banana. Mix together sugar and cinnamon and sprinkle over banana. Broil until brown and bubbly.

Nutrient Analysis: 1 serving
168 Calories, 5 g Fat, 5 g Protein, 27 g Carbohydrate, 3 g Fiber, 185 mg Sodium, 0 mg Cholesterol,
2 g Sat Fat.
Exchanges: 1 bread, 1 fruit, 1 fat.

CINNAMON ALMOND TOAST

Here is a variation of an old standard--cinnamon toast. Whole grain bread and almonds add fiber, while light margarine lowers the fat.

Serves 1

2   slices whole grain bread
2   teaspoons light tub margarine
2   tablespoons light brown sugar (or equivalent sugar substitute)
1/4   teaspoon cinnamon
2   teaspoons slivered almonds

Toast bread and spread with light margarine. Combine brown sugar and cinnamon; sprinkle over toast. Top with slivered almonds. Broil until almonds are light golden brown.

Nutrient Analysis: 1 serving
314 Calories, 10 g Fat, 6 g Protein, 53 g Carbohydrate, 3 g Fiber, 320 mg Sodium, 0 mg Cholesterol,
3 g Sat Fat.
Exchanges: 2 fruit, 2 bread, 2 fat.

TRAIL MIX

For variety, add 2 tablespoons mini chocolate chips to the mix

2 1/4 cups; 4 servings

1   **cup low-fat granola**
1   **cup dried fruit, diced**
1/4   **cup slivered almonds**

Mix all ingredients together in medium bowl. Store in an airtight container for up to 2 weeks.

Nutrient Analysis: 1 serving
261 Calories, 6 g Fat, 4 g Protein, 32 g Carbohydrates, 6 g Fiber 36 mg Sodium, 0 mg Cholesterol
1 g Sat Fat.
Exchanges: 2 fruit, 1 bread, 1 fat

PAN FRIED PEAR FRENCH TOAST

We haven't gone too far in calling this a work of art. Try it and see what you think.

Serves 1

1	teaspoon light stick margarine
1	small, semi-ripened pear, peeled and cored
1	teaspoon sugar (or equivalent sugar subsititute)
1	whole egg
3	tablespoons skim milk
1/8	teaspoon cinnamon
2	slices good quality white or whole wheat bread

Vegetable cooking spray

Cut pear into 12 thin slices. Melt margarine over medium heat in small skillet. Add pear slices and cook until golden. Add sugar and mix until sugar melts. Set aside and wipe skillet clean.

Beat together egg, skim milk and cinnamon and dip bread in egg mixture. Coat skillet with vegetable cooking spray and arrange the 12 slices into two fan-shaped patterns. Place a slice of bread on each pear fan. Press each slice down lightly with spatula about 10 seconds so that pears adhere to the bread. Cook until golden brown (about 3 minutes). Flip carefully and cook the other side.

Nutrient Analysis: 1 serving
347 Calories, 9 g Fat, 14 g Protein, 51 g Carbohydrate, 8 g Fiber, 394 mg Sodium, 207 mg Cholesterol, 3 g Sat Fat.
Exchanges: 2 fruit, 2 bread, 1 meat, 2 fat.

FRUIT PIZZA

This dish unites fruit, dairy, and grain foods. Personalize it for each member of the family with different fruits: strawberries, peaches, kiwi, grapes, etc.

Serves 1.

1	6-inch whole wheat pita bread
3	teaspoons brown sugar (or equivalent sugar substitute)
1/3	cup low-fat ricotta cheese
1/2	cup mixed fresh fruit of your choice (eg. strawberries, kiwi, bananas, etc.)

Preheat oven to 450° F. Toast pita bread for 4 - 5 minutes until crisp. Mix one teaspoon brown sugar (or equivalent sugar substitute) with ricotta cheese and spread on pita. Top with fruit of choice. Sprinkle with remaining two teaspoons brown sugar. Bake 5 - 6 more minutes and serve.

Nutrient Analysis: 1 serving (made with 1/4 cup sliced strawberries and 1/4 cup chopped kiwi)
364 Calories, 7 g Fat, 16 g Protein, 57 g Carbohydrate, 6 g Fiber, 416 mg Sodium, 24 mg Cholesterol,
4 g Sat Fat.
Exchanges: 2 fruit, 2 bread, 1 meat, 1/2 fat.

HEARTY OATMEAL

Put a little zing (as well as fiber) in your oatmeal. Because instant oatmeal is used, this recipe is a real quickie. Pack some in a small zip-lock bag and keep in your desk or briefcase for those times you can't have breakfast at home. For the sodium conscious, use brands having around 5 milligrams of sodium in a one-ounce package (see page 217 for suggested brands).

Serves 1

1	package (1-ounce) instant oatmeal, plain
3	tablespoons Grape Nuts® cereal
2	tablespoons raisins
2	tablespoons slivered almonds

Mix ingredients in a bowl. Add about 2/3 cup boiling water and stir.

MICROWAVE DIRECTIONS: Mix all ingredients together with 2/3 cup water in small glass bowl and heat 1 - 1 1/2 minutes on high.

Nutrient Analysis: 1 serving
330 Calories, 10 g Fat, 11 g Protein, 53 g Carbohydrate, 5 g Fiber, 430 mg Sodium, 0 mg Cholesterol, 2 g Sat Fat.
Exchanges: 1 fruit, 3 bread, 1/2 fat.

Our approach to inceasing daily fiber intake
is to start your day with a cereal that provides
at least 3 grams of fiber/serving.

The Authors

RAISIN RICE CEREAL WITH ALMONDS

Like hot breakfast cereals but want something out of the ordinary? This combines the nutty flavors of rice and almonds with every creamy spoonful. As a timesaver, use left-over rice from a previous meal.

Serves 1

2/3	cup cooked brown rice
1/2	cup skim milk
2	tablespoons slivered almonds
1	tablespoon raisins
1/4	teaspoon cinnamon
1	teaspoon brown sugar (or equivalent sugar substitute)

Warm rice in microwave till steaming (about 1 minute); stir in remaining ingredients.

Nutrient Analysis: 1 serving
330 Calories, 10 g Fat, 14 g Protein, 48 g Carbohydrate, 3 g Fiber, 69 mg Sodium, 3 mg Cholesterol,
2 g Sat Fat.
Exchanges: 1/2 milk, 1 fruit, 2 bread, 1 fat.

HOT FRUITED GRANOLA WITH CHERRY YOGURT GARNISH

Experiment with this novel approach to granola. "Pro-carb connecting" is easy when you combine it with 1 1/2 cups of skim milk.

Serves 1

3/4   cup low-fat granola (see page 228 for recommended brands)
1/4   cup evaporated skim milk
1 1/2 tablespoons chopped dried fruit (eg. apples, cherries, or apricots)
2   tablespoons lowfat cherry flavored yogurt

Place cereal, milk, and dried fruit in a microwave safe bowl. Cover with plastic wrap and make a small slit in center of plastic wrap to vent. Heat for 30 seconds on high. Stir, replace plastic wrap, and heat for another 30 seconds on high, or until cereal becomes soft. Top with yogurt and serve.

Nutrient Analysis: 1 serving.
271 Calories, 3 g Fat, 7 g Protein, 54 g Carbohydrate, 3 g Fiber, 118 mg Sodium, 2 mg Cholesterol,
0 g Sat Fat.
Exchanges: 1/2 milk, 2 fruit, 2 bread.

"ORZO" IT SEEMS CEREAL

This delightful concoction of orzo (a rice-shaped pasta found in most supermarkets), carrots, bananas, and nuts gives you enough vitamin A for the entire day! A "pro-carb connection" is made with the addition of 1 1/2 cups of skim milk.

Serves 1

1/3   cup dry orzo (or rice)
2-3   cups water
1/4   cup chopped raw carrot

1/2   large banana
1   teaspoon sugar (or equivalent sugar substitute)
1/2   teaspoon butter
1   tablespoon chopped honey roast peanuts
Pinch of salt

Cook orzo or rice in 2-3 cups water for 8 minutes. Stir in carrot; cook for another 3 minutes or until tender. Drain and set aside. Slice banana, and place in cereal bowl. Add orzo mixture, sugar, butter, nuts, and salt, then mix till blended.

Nutrient Analysis: 1 serving
323 Calories, 7 g Fat, 6 g Protein, 58 g Carbohydrate, 3 g Fiber, 92 mg Sodium, 6 mg Cholesterol,
1 g Sat Fat.
Exchanges: 2 fruit, 2 bread, 1 fat.

OAT BRAN WITH PEACH BUTTER

Several taste testers and colleagues praised this recipe very highly--even those that never eat hot cereal!

Serves 1

2   fresh peaches, peeled, sliced, and pitted
1/4   cup water
1   tablespoon sugar (or equivalent sugar substitute)

1/4   cup uncooked oat bran (Health Valley® brand if available)
1/2   cup water

Place peach slices, water, and sugar in small saucepan. Cook, covered, over medium heat until peaches are very soft. Mash peaches with fork. Set aside. Cook oat bran in water according to package directions for single serving. When done, mix cooked peaches into oat bran and serve.

Nutrient Analysis: 1 serving
220 Calories, 2 g Fat, 6 g Protein, 45 g Carbohydrate, 6 g Fiber, 4 mg Sodium, 0 mg Cholesterol,
0 g Sat Fat.
Exchanges: 2 fruit, 1 bread.

WAFFLE SANDWICH

Want an easy to eat, energy-packed breakfast? If the kids are running late, this is something they can eat while waiting for the bus. Sodium watchers, please be alert. This meal is quite high in sodium because of the waffles. Balance the rest of your day accordingly.

Serves 1

1   **tablespoon chunky peanut butter**
2   **tablespoons mashed banana**
1   **teaspoon honey**
2   **light frozen waffles, toasted (see page 228 for recommended brands)**

Combine peanut butter, banana, and honey in a small bowl.

Spread on toasted waffles.

Nutrient Analysis: 1 serving
249 Calories, 9 g Fat, 7 g Protein, 439 g Carbohydrate, 8 g Fiber, 0 mg Cholesterol, 558 mg Sodium,
3 g Sat Fat.
Exchanges: 1 fruit, 2 bread, 1 fat.

*A balanced meal is as important
as a balanced checkbook.*

SHRIMP TACO

Yes, shrimp can be eaten for breakfast. Pop it in the microwave or use leftover shrimp to make this super-quick.

Serves 1

1   **corn tortilla**
2   **ounces leftover cooked shrimp**

Warm tortilla in microwave for a few seconds, and roll shrimp in tortilla. Serve with 2 teaspoons cocktail sauce if desired.

Variations: Instead of shrimp, use cooked lean roast beef, turkey breast, or leftover cooked whitefish (eg. cod, haddock, trout, or perch).

Nutrient Analysis: 1 serving (prepared with shrimp, no cocktail sauce)
123 Calories, 2 g Fat, 14 g Protein, 13 g Carbohydrate, 180 mg Sodium, 111 mg Cholesterol,
0 g Sat Fat.
Exchanges: 1 bread, 1 meat.

Shrimp is the most popular crustacean
in this country. Although fairly high in cholesterol,
shrimp is very low in fat.

CHICKEN PITA POCKET

If you enjoy chicken fajitas, you'll love this recipe. Create another superb "pro-carb" connection menu by accompanying this sandwich with skim milk and fruit.

Serves 1

1/2	6-inch pita bread
3	ounces leftover cooked, skinned chicken breast
1	tablespoon picante sauce
1	tomato slice
1	small avocado slice

Shredded lettuce

Fill pita bread with chicken first, then the other ingredients in whatever order desired.

Nutrient Analysis: 1 serving (with 1/2 6-inch pita)
211 Calories, 5 g Fat, 23 g Protein, 19 g Carbohydrate, 347 mg Sodium, 48 mg Cholesterol,
2 g Sat Fat.
Exchanges: 1 bread, 2 1/2 meat.

MEGA MUFFIN SANDWICH

Egg substitute and light cheese produce a slimmed down version of the popular fast food sandwich. For sodium sleuths, Oscar Meyer® or Weight Watchers® low salt ham drops the sodium content per serving to 332 mg. With a glass of juice, this becomes a really boss "pro-carb connection"!

Serves 1

1   **English muffin (or two slices whole grain bread for sodium watchers)**
1   **slice Canadian bacon**
Vegetable cooking spray (1 3-second spray)
1/4   **cup egg substitute, thawed**
1   **ounce shredded light cheddar cheese**

Toast muffin. Warm Canadian bacon in microwave for 10 seconds. Spray nonstick skillet with vegetable cooking spray, then scramble the egg substitute. Place bacon on bottom half of muffin. Top with egg and shredded cheese. Broil just until cheese melts (less than 1 minute). Top with other English muffin half. Serve warm.

Nutrient Analysis: 1 serving
282 Calories, 8 g Fat, 23 g Protein, 28 g Carbohydrate, 948 mg Sodium, 33 mg Cholesterol,
4 g Sat Fat.
Exchanges: 2 bread, 2 meat.

BREAKFAST PIZZA SUPREME

If you decide to bake instead of microwave, put the cheese over the toppings, and not vice versa. This recipe does have quite a bit of sodium because of the spaghetti sauce, cheese, ham, and English muffin. To cut back, substitute low-sodium spaghetti sauce, low salt ham, 2 tablespoons part skim mozzarella cheese, and 2 slices whole wheat bread in the recipe.

Serves 1

2	tablespoons bottled meatless spaghetti sauce
2	English muffin halves
3	tablespoons shredded part skim mozzarella cheese
1	teaspoon grated Parmesan cheese
1	slice Canadian bacon, chopped
1	tablespoon chopped fresh mushrooms
2	teaspoons chopped bell pepper

Spread spaghetti sauce over English muffin halves. Sprinkle with mozzarella and Parmesan cheese, then add toppings. Microwave for 30 seconds on high or bake in 350° F. oven for 5 minutes.

Nutrient Analysis: 1 serving
282 Calories, 8 g Fat, 17 g Protein, 34 g Carbohydrate, 1087 mg Sodium, 27 mg Cholesterol,
4 g Sat Fat.
Exchanges: 1 vegetable, 2 bread, 2 meat.

SOFT TACO WITH BACON, EGG AND CORN

Corn adds fiber to this quick sandwich.

Serves 1

Vegetable cooking spray (1 3-second spray)
1/2   cup frozen egg substitute, thawed
2   slices leftover cooked turkey bacon, crumbled
1/3   cup leftover cooked whole kernel corn (no salt added)
1   large flour tortilla
1/3   cup chopped tomato
Lettuce leaf

In a small skillet coated with cooking spray, scramble egg substitute over medium heat until almost set. Add turkey bacon pieces and corn, then finish cooking until egg substitute is set.

Spread the mixture over the tortilla; roll up and serve with chopped tomato and lettuce.

Nutrient Analysis: 1 serving
307 Calories, 9 g Fat, 17 g Protein, 47 g Carbohydrate, 3 g Fiber, 650 mg Sodium, 20 mg Cholesterol,
2 g Sat Fat.
Exchanges: 1 vegetable, 3 bread, 1 meat.

CHEESY BROCCOLI SOUP

A hearty and satisfying breakfast by itself. Those on sodium-restricted diets should savor this soup only occasionally.

Serves 2

1   can (10 3/4-ounces) low-fat cream of broccoli soup
10 3/4 fluid ounces skim milk
3/4   cup shredded fat-free cheddar cheese

Combine soup and milk in medium saucepan. Bring to a boil over medium heat, then simmer for approximately 3-5 minutes. Remove from heat, and stir in the cheese.

Nutrient Analysis: 1 serving
205 Calories, 3 g Fat, 16 g Protein, 24 g Carbohydrate, 905 mg Sodium, 22 mg Cholesterol,
1 g Sat Fat.
Exchanges: 1/2 milk, 2 1/2 bread.

BREAKFAST QUESADILLA

A quick and filling breakfast with Mexican origins. A "pro-carb" connection in and of it-self.

Serves 1

2   **8-inch flour tortillas**
3   **tablespoons shredded light Monterey Jack cheese**
3   **tablespoons shredded fat-free cheddar cheese**
1/4   **cup TURKEY CHORIZO (page 186), cooked**
Vegetable cooking spray (2 3-second sprays)

Preheat oven to 350° F. Evenly distribute the cheeses and turkey chorizo over one tortilla, then cover with the other tortilla (this is now a quesadilla). Coat baking sheet with one 3-second spray of vegetable cooking spray, then place quesadilla on baking sheet.

Bake for 4 minutes, then spray the top of the quesadilla for one 3-second spray of vegetable cooking spray. Turn over, and bake for another 4 minutes. Remove from oven, and cut into 4 wedges with pizza cutter or sharp knife.

Nutrient Analysis: 1 serving
373 Calories, 11 g Fat, 21 g Protein, 48 g Carbohydrate, 739 mg Sodium, 36 mg Cholesterol,
4 g Sat Fat.
Exchanges: 3 bread, 1 1/2 meat, 2 fat.

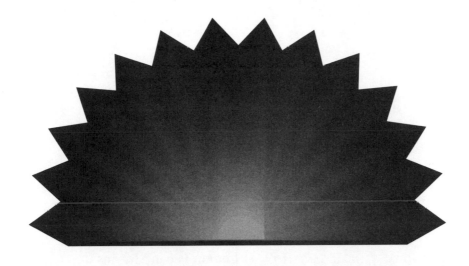

Quick
Recipes

If you have to work before breakfast,
get your breakfast first.

Josh Billings

Quick Recipes

FRUITY BREAKFAST TOSTADA

Serves 1

1/4   cup sliced fresh strawberries
1/4   cup peeled, diced fresh kiwifruit
1/2   teaspoon sugar (or equivalent sugar substitute)

1   8-inch flour tortilla
1/2   teaspoon light tub margarine, melted
1   teaspoon confectioners sugar
1 1/2 teaspoons sugar (or equivalent sugar substitute)
1   tablespoon low-fat ricotta cheese
1/2   tablespoon light cream cheese

Mix fresh fruits and sugar together and set aside.

Heat small nonstick skillet. Brush both sides of tortilla with margarine and cook each side until crisp and golden brown. Sprinkle with confectioners sugar and top with fresh fruit mixture. Combine sugar and cheeses. Place dollop of cheese mixture atop fruit and serve.

Nutrient Analysis: 1 serving
251 Calories, 7 g Fat, 6 g Protein, 41 g Carbohydrate, 3 g Fiber, 244 mg Sodium, 11 mg Cholesterol,
1 g Sat Fat.
Exchanges: 2 fruit, 1 bread, 1 fat.

GRANOLA STUFFED PEAR WITH LEMON BREAKFAST CREAM

A fancy breakfast treat that is very easy to make.

Serves 1

1   **medium fresh pear**
1/4   **cup low-fat granola**
1/2   **teaspoon peanut butter**
1/8   **teaspoon nutmeg**
1/8   **teaspoon cinnamon**
1   **teaspoon brown sugar (or equivalent sugar substitute)**
1   **teaspoon raisins**
2   **tablespoons LEMON BREAKFAST CREAM (page 105)**

Slice top off pear. With spoon, scoop out pulp, discarding seeds. Leave a 1/2 inch edge around pear shell. Set aside.

In small bowl, mix pulp with granola, peanut butter, spices, raisins and brown sugar. Fill pear with granola mixture. Place bottom side down in small, shallow baking dish and fill with 1-inch of water. Bake at 400° F. for 10 minutes. Top with LEMON BREAKFAST CREAM.

Nutrient Analysis: 1 serving
264 Calories, 5 g Fat, 5 g Protein, 50 g Carbohydrate, 5 g Fiber, 96 mg Sodium, 18 mg Cholesterol,
2 g Sat Fat.
Exchanges: 2 fruit, 1 bread, 1 fat.

PEANUT BUTTER & JELLY GRANOLA BARS

These high energy bars are made to order for your PB & J fans. Have children mix these with their hands. Besides being a super breakfast, they are great to tuck away in a lunch-box or to keep handy as an after school snack.

8 bars

2   **cups uncooked oats**
1/3   **cup peanut butter (creamy or crunchy)**
1/2   **cup grape jelly (or low-sugar grape spread)**

In medium bowl, mix all ingredients together thoroughly.

Spread in lightly greased 8-inch square pan. Bake at 350° F. for 20 - 25 minutes. Allow to cool at least 10 minutes before cutting into bars.

Nutrient Analysis: 1 bar
195 Calories, 6 g Fat, 6 g Protein, 28 g Carbohydrate, 56 mg Sodium, 0 mg Cholesterol,
1 g Sat Fat.
Exchanges: 1 fruit, 1 bread, 1 fat.

BREAKFAST SHORTCAKE

Dessert for breakfast, you ask? It's great for a brunch with family and friends. Garnish with a dollop of light non-dairy whipped topping.

Serves 12

SHORTCAKE:
2 cups LIGHT BISCUIT MIX (page 184)
1/3 cup sugar
3/4 cup nonfat plain yogurt
1/4 cup skim milk
1 teaspoon vanilla

STRAWBERRIES AND CREAM FILLING:
4 tablespoons sugar (or equivalent sugar substitute)
3 cups fresh strawberries, sliced
1 cup lowfat vanilla yogurt
1/4 cup light sour cream
1 teaspoon vanilla extract
2 teaspoons sugar (or equivalent sugar substitute)

Place shortcake ingredients in large bowl and stir until just combined. Pour into two greased and floured 8-inch round cake pans. Bake in 425° F. oven for 20 minutes, or until toothpick inserted in center comes out clean.

Sprinkle 4 tablespoons sugar over strawberries in one bowl. Combine yogurt, sour cream, vanilla, and 2 teaspoons sugar in another bowl. Remove shortcake from pan by running a knife around the edge and inverting.

Spread half of the strawberry mixture on one layer of shortcake. Place the other shortcake layer on top. Top with remaining strawberry mixture. Before serving, top with yogurt and sour cream mixture.

Nutrient Analysis: 1 serving (made with sugar, without whipped topping)
173 Calories, 4 g Fat, 4 g Protein, 30 g Carbohydrate, 212 mg Sodium, 2 mg Cholesterol,
0 g Sat Fat.
Exchanges: 1 fruit, 1 bread, 1 fat.

CINNAMON DANISH ROLLS

8 rolls

Vegetable cooking spray (2 3-second sprays)
1/2   cup brown sugar
1   package (11-ounces) Pillsbury Soft White Breadsticks®
1   tablespoon stick margarine, melted
1/3   cup raisins
1   teaspoon cinnamon

Preheat oven to 350° F. Spray 9-inch pie pan with cooking spray. Sprinkle with half of the brown sugar.

Roll each piece of dough (end over end) into a pinwheel shape, place and press into pan. Rolls will touch each other. Mix together melted margarine, remaining brown sugar, raisins and cinnamon. Drizzle over rolls. Bake in oven for 15-20 minutes, or until golden.

Nutrient Analysis: 1 roll
156 Calories, 3 g Fat, 3 g Protein, 23 g Carbohydrate, 250 mg Sodium, 1 mg Cholesterol,
0 g Sat Fat.
Exchanges: 1 fruit, 1 bread.

CINNAMON CRISPS WITH APPLESAUCE

Kids love this recipe. Give them their own bowl of warmed applesauce for dipping.

Serves 4

1	tablespoon hot water
1/2	teaspoon vanilla extract

3	tablespoons sugar (or equivalent sugar substitute)
1/2	teaspoon cinnamon

4   6-inch flour tortillas
Butter-flavored vegetable cooking spray (6 3-second sprays)
3/4   cup unsweetened chunky applesauce

Combine water and vanilla in small bowl. Set aside. Mix sugar and cinnamon together in another small bowl. Cut each tortilla into 6 triangles.

Brush both sides of tortilla triangles with water-vanilla mixture, then sprinkle both sides with sugar-cinnamon mixture. Place tortilla triangles in one layer on baking sheet coated with vegetable cooking spray. Bake in 450° F. oven for about 5 minutes or until crispy. Serve applesauce as a dip.

Nutrient Analysis: 1 serving
144 Calories, 3 g Fat, 2 g Protein, 27 g Carbohydrate, 111 mg Sodium, 0 mg Cholesterol,
0 g Sat Fat.
Exchanges: 1 bread, 1 fruit.

STREUSEL BREAKFAST BARS

Serve these instead of doughnuts at your next office meeting.

16 bars

Vegetable cooking spray (2 3-second sprays)
1   cup brown sugar
1/2   cup light tub margarine
3/4   cup white flour
1/2   cup whole wheat flour
1 1/4 cups uncooked rolled oats
3/4   cup sugar-free preserves, at room temperature

Preheat oven to 400° F. Coat a 13 x 9 x 2-inch pan with vegetable cooking spray.

In large bowl, beat brown sugar and margarine until light and fluffy. Add flours and oats to sugar-margarine mixture; mix at low speed until crumbly.

Reserve 1 cup for topping; press remaining crumb mixture in bottom of prepared pan. Spread with preserves. Top with remaining crumb mixture. Bake at 400° F. for 18-25 minutes or until light golden brown. Cool completely.

Nutrient Analysis: 1 bar
148 Calories, 3 g Fat, 2 g Protein, 28 g Carbohydrate, 72 mg Sodium, 0 mg Cholesterol,
0 g Sat Fat.
Exchanges: 1 fruit, 1 bread.

SPICED APPLE TOAST

As attractive as it is delicious. When your family tires of everyday toast, surprise them with this new approach.

Serves 4

1	tablespoon light tub margarine
2	apples, unpeeled, cored and thinly sliced
1/3	cup orange juice
4	teaspoons brown sugar (or equivalent sugar substitute)
1/2	teaspoon ground cinnamon
4	slices whole wheat bread, toasted
2	teaspoons sugar (or equivalent sugar substitute)
Vegetable cooking spray	

In a medium non-stick skillet, melt margarine. Add apples, orange juice, brown sugar, and cinnamon; cook over medium- high heat until apples are tender (about 4 minutes), stirring occasionally. Drain and reserve cooking liquid, which should resemble syrup. Allow apples to cool a few minutes.

Place toast on a baking sheet coated with vegetable cooking spray. Arrange apples atop each piece of toast, then sprinkle with 1/2 teaspoon sugar. Bake in 450° F. oven about 4 - 5 minutes or until bread is crisp. Drizzle the reserved liquid over the slices and serve with knife and fork.

Nutrient Analysis: 4 servings
141 Calories, 3 g Fat, 2 g Protein, 27 g Carbohydrate, 3 g Fiber, 172 mg Sodium, 0 mg Cholesterol,
1 g Sat Fat.
Exchanges: 1 fruit, 1 bread.

FRENCH TOAST

Has that good old-fashioned flavor.

Serves 2

4   slices day-old white or whole wheat bread
1/4   cup egg substitute, thawed
1   whole egg, beaten
2/3   cup 1% milk
1   teaspoon real vanilla extract
1   tablespoon butter (the amount is OK for this recipe)

Dip bread slices in a mixture of egg substitute, whole egg, milk, and vanilla extract. Set aside.

Melt butter in 10-inch cast iron skillet. Place bread slices in skillet. Cook bread on the first side over medium heat until well-browned. Turn the bread over and continue to cook on the other side until well-browned.

Nutrient Analysis: 1 serving (2 slices)
247 Calories, 9 g Fat, 13 g Protein, 29 g Carbohydrate, 416 mg Sodium, 129 mg Cholesterol,
6 g Sat Fat.
Exchanges: 2 bread, 1 meat, 1 fat.

PINEAPPLE UPSIDE DOWN FRENCH TOAST

For best results, use bread that is at least one day old.

Serves 4

4   slices day-old white or whole wheat bread
1/4   cup egg substitute, thawed
1   whole egg, beaten
2/3   cup 1% milk
1   teaspoon real vanilla extract

1   tablespoon butter (this amount is OK for the recipe)
4   tablespoons brown sugar
4   canned unsweetened pineapple rings, drained well

Dip bread slices in a mixture of egg substitute, whole egg, milk, and vanilla extract. Melt butter in 10-inch cast iron skillet. Place bread slices in skillet. Add one tablespoon of brown sugar on one side of each bread slice, spreading to coat the entire slice of bread. Lay a pineapple ring on top of the brown sugar.

Cook bread on the first side over medium heat until well-browned. Turn the bread over and continue to cook on the other side for approximately 5 minutes, or until well-browned and the brown sugar is melted. Serve immediately.

Nutrient Analysis: 1 serving
187 Calories, 5 g Fat, 5 g Protein, 29 g Carbohydrate, 201 mg Sodium, 65 mg Cholesterol,
3 g Sat Fat.
Exchanges: 1 fruit, 1 bread, 1 meat.

"BY DAWN'S EARLY LIGHT" MUFFINS

12 muffins

2   cups LIGHT MUFFIN MIX (page 183)
1/4   cup egg substitute, thawed
1   cup skim milk
1   tablespoon canola oil
Vegetable cooking spray (3 3-second sprays)

Place muffin mix in medium bowl; then add egg substitute, milk, and oil. Stir just until combined. Coat muffin tins with vegetable cooking spray. Fill each 2/3 full.

Bake in 425° F. oven for 15 minutes, or until toothpick inserted in center comes out clean.

Variations: Add 1 tablespoon raisins, 2 teaspoons mini chocolate chip morsels, or 1 tablespoon chopped dried apricots. Just let your imagination run wild (but do tame any added fat)!

Nutrient Analysis: 1 muffin (plain)
99 Calories, 2 g Fat, 4 g Protein, 17 g Carbohydrate, 204 mg Sodium, 0 mg Cholesterol,
0 g Sat Fat.
Exchanges: 1 bread.

Variation: BLUEBERRY MUFFINS

12 muffins

Follow recipe for "BY DAWN'S EARLY LIGHT" MUFFINS on preceding page, adding:

1-2   cups fresh or frozen (thawed and drained) blueberries to batter
3   tablespoons of sugar.

Nutrient Analysis. 1 muffin (from recipe using 1 cup berries)
118 Calories, 2 g Fat, 3 g Protein, 22 g Carbohydrate, 204 mg Sodium, 0 mg Cholesterol,
0 g Sat Fat.
Exchanges: 1/2 fruit, 1 bread.

Eating is not merely a material pleasure.
Eating well gives a spectacular joy to life
and contributes immensely to goodwill
and happy companionship. It is of great
importance to the morale.

Elsa Schiaparelli

BANANA MUFFINS

Bananas are a prime source of potassium. Their sweetness helps replace some of the sugar. These muffins can be frozen up to three months.

12 muffins

1 3/4 cups LIGHT MUFFIN MIX (page 183)
3   tablespoons sugar
2   tablespoons oil
1/2   cup egg substitute, thawed
2   tablespoons skim milk
1   cup mashed bananas (2-3 bananas)
Vegetable cooking spray (3 3-second sprays)

In medium bowl, combine muffin mix and sugar. Add other ingredients, stirring just until combined.

Coat muffin tins with vegetable cooking spray. Fill each 2/3 full. Bake in 425° F. oven for 15 minutes, or until toothpick inserted in center comes out clean.

Nutrient Analysis: 1 muffin
120 Calories, 3 g Fat, 3 g Protein, 22 g Carbohydrate, 176 mg Sodium, 0 mg Cholesterol,
0 g Sat Fat.
Exchanges: 1 fruit, 1 bread.

BANANA BRAN MUFFINS

Since this sugar-free recipe makes 24 muffins, we recommend freezing leftovers. Place in a plastic container or zip-lock bag for storage. Just pop in the microwave on high for 30 seconds to reheat.

24 muffins

2	cups bran cereal
1/2	cup canola oil
1	cup boiling water

1/2	cup egg substitute, thawed
2	cups mashed bananas (about 4 or 5)
1/4	cup skim milk

2 1/4	cups whole wheat flour
2	teaspoons baking powder
1/2	teaspoon salt

Vegetable cooking spray (3 3-second sprays)

Preheat oven to 425° F. In a large bowl, combine the bran cereal, oil, and boiling water. Allow to cool until lukewarm. Add the egg substitute, mashed bananas, and milk; stir well. In another bowl, combine the flour, baking powder and salt. Add this to the cereal and banana mixture and stir just enough to mix. Coat muffin tins with vegetable cooking spray and fill each 2/3 full. Bake 15-20 minutes, or until toothpick inserted in center comes out clean.

Nutrient Analysis: 1 muffin
157 Calories, 5 g Fat, 3 g Protein, 25 g Carbohydrate, 4 g Fiber, 157 mg Sodium, 0 mg Cholesterol,
0 g Sat Fat.
Exchanges: 1/2 fruit, 1 bread, 1 fat.

PUMPKIN MUFFINS

Do you have a hard time including vitamin A-rich vegetables into the family meal plan? Pumpkin is an excellent source of Vitamin A; 2 muffins provide 85% of the recommended Vitamin A intake for children.

12 muffins

1 3/4 cups **LIGHT MUFFIN MIX (page 183)**
2   **teaspoons pumpkin pie spice**
2   **tablespoons canola oil**
1/2   **cup egg substitute, thawed or 2 whole eggs**
2   **tablespoons skim milk**
1/4   **cup molasses**
1   **cup canned pumpkin**
Vegetable cooking spray (3 3-second sprays)

In medium bowl, combine muffin mix and pumpkin pie spice.

Add remaining ingredients and stir until just combined. Coat muffin tins with vegetable cooking spray, then fill each 2/3 full. Bake in 425° F. oven for 15 - 20 minutes, or until toothpick inserted in center comes out clean.

Nutrient Analysis: 1 muffin (made with egg substitute)
116 Calories, 3 g Fat, 4 g Protein, 19 g Carbohydrate, 188 mg Sodium, 0 mg Cholesterol,
0 g Sat Fat.
Exchanges: 1/2 fruit, 1 bread.

LEMON PECAN MUFFINS

A lower fat variation to lemon pecan cake. Toasting the pecans offers a richer flavor.

12 muffins

1/4	cup toasted chopped pecans
2	cups LIGHT MUFFIN MIX (page 183)
1/2	cup sugar
2	teaspoons grated lemon rind
3	tablespoons fresh squeezed lemon juice
2/3	cup skim milk
1	tablespoon canola oil
1/4	cup egg substitute, thawed

Vegetable cooking spray (3 3-second sprays)

Preheat oven to 425° F. To toast pecans, place under broiler for about 30 seconds or until browned.

Combine pecans, dry mix, sugar, and lemon rind in medium bowl. Add individual liquid ingredients to dry mixture. Stir just until moistened. Coat muffin tins with vegetable cooking spray and fill each 2/3 full. Bake for 15-18 minutes, or until toothpick inserted in center comes out clean.

Nutrient Analysis: 1 muffin
140 Calories, 3 g Fat, 4 g Protein, 25 g Carbohydrate, 200 mg Sodium, 0 mg Cholesterol,
0 g Sat Fat.
Exchanges: 1 fruit, 1 bread.

BROCCOLI CHEESE MUFFINS

There's nothing like 'em at brunch!

12 muffins

2/3	**cup cooked, chopped broccoli**
2/3	**cup shredded light cheddar cheese**
1/4	**cup egg substitute, thawed**
1	**cup skim milk**
2	**cups LIGHT MUFFIN MIX (page 183)**

Vegetable cooking spray (3 3-second sprays)

Preheat oven to 425° F. Combine broccoli, cheese, egg substitute and milk. Add broccoli-cheese mixture to dry muffin mix. Stir just until moistened.

Coat muffin tins with vegetable cooking spray. Fill each 2/3 full. Bake for 15-18 minutes, or until toothpick inserted in center comes out clean.

Nutrient Analysis: 1 muffin
118 Calories, 2 g Fat, 6 g Protein, 19 g Carbohydrate, 245 mg Sodium, 13 mg Cholesterol,
1 g Sat Fat.
Exchanges: 1 bread, 1/2 meat.

FLUFFY BISCUITS

13 biscuits

2   **cups LIGHT BISCUIT MIX (page 184)**
2   **teaspoons sugar**
1   **cup nonfat plain yogurt**
2   **tablespoons skim milk**

Preheat oven to 425° F. In medium bowl, combine biscuit mix and sugar. Stir in yogurt and skim milk until just blended.

Turn onto floured surface and knead 4 times. Roll out to 1/2-inch thickness and cut with biscuit cutter. Place on ungreased cookie sheet. Bake for 8-10 minutes or until golden.

Nutrient Analysis: 1 biscuit
97 Calories, 3 g Fat, 3 g Protein, 15 g Carbohydrate, 183 mg Sodium, 0 mg Cholesterol,
0 g Sat Fat.
Exchanges: 1 bread, 1/2 fat.

Subdue your appetites, my dears,
and you' ve conquered human nature.

Charles Dickens

SPEEDY CHEDDAR BISCUITS

Biting into these "fresh from the oven" biscuits is a heavenly experience. Serve alone, with juice at breakfast or with your favorite chili or soup later in the day.

13 biscuits

2   cups **LIGHT BISCUIT MIX (page 184)**
2/3   **cup skim milk**
1/2   **cup shredded light cheddar cheese**
       (choose a brand with no more than 3 grams fat per ounce)

Preheat oven to 425°F. In medium bowl, combine all ingredients and stir until just blended.

Turn onto floured surface and knead 4 times. Roll out to 1/2-inch thickness and cut with biscuit cutter. Place on ungreased cookie sheet. Bake for 8-10 minutes or until golden brown.

Nutrient Analysis: 1 biscuit
95 Calories, 3 g Fat, 3 g Protein, 13 g Carbohydrate, 240 mg Sodium, 10 mg Cholesterol,
1 g Sat Fat.
Exchanges: 1 bread, 1/2 fat.

TURKEY SAUSAGE AND CHEESE BISCUITS

For "pro-carb" connections, plan on having 2 biscuits with a glass of skim milk and juice. Sodium watchers: use low-sodium, light cheese in the recipe.

12 biscuits

1/4	pound raw, ground turkey sausage
2	cups LIGHT BISCUIT MIX (page 184)
1/4	cup shredded light cheddar cheese
	(choose a brand with no more than 3 grams of fat per ounce)
2/3	cup skim milk

Preheat oven to 425° F. Brown turkey sausage, breaking it up into small pieces with cooking utensil; drain off the fat.

In medium bowl, combine turkey sausage, biscuit mix, shredded cheese, and milk. Stir just until blended.

Turn onto floured surface and knead 4 times. Roll out to 1/2-inch thickness and cut with biscuit cutter. Place on ungreased cookie sheet. Bake for 8-10 minutes or until golden brown.

Nutrient Analysis: 1 biscuit
118 Calories, 4 g Fat, 4 g Protein, 14 g Carbohydrate, 300 mg Sodium, 9 mg Cholesterol, 1 g Sat Fat.
Exchanges: 1 bread, 1 fat

LIGHT CORNBREAD
Good anytime of the day.

Serves 8

1 3/4 cups self-rising cornmeal
2   tablespoons sugar
1   whole egg or 1/4 cup egg substitute, thawed
2   tablespoons canola oil
1 1/4 cups skim milk
Vegetable cooking spray (2 3-second sprays)

Preheat oven to 400° F. Place dry ingredients in a bowl and mix with fork. Add egg, oil, and milk and mix until just combined. Pour into 8-inch square baking pan coated with vegetable cooking spray. Bake for 20 minutes or until toothpick inserted in center comes out clean.

Ingredient Note: If you do not have self-rising cornmeal, substitute 1 cup flour, 3/4 cup cornmeal, 1 tablesoon baking powder and 1/2 teaspoon salt.

Nutrient Analysis: 1 serving (self-rising cornmeal)
176 Calories, 4 g Fat, 5 g Protein, 29 g Carbohydrate, 361 mg Sodium, 27 mg Cholesterol,
1 g Sat Fat.
Exchanges: 1 1/2 bread, 1 fat.

Nutrient Analysis: 1 serving (flour/cornmeal)
156 calories, 4 g Fat, 5 g Protein, 23 g Carbohydrate, 322 mg Sodium, 27 mg Cholesterol,
1 g Sat Fat.
Exchanges: 1 1/2 bread, 1 fat.

OATMEAL RAISIN PANCAKES

These make a grand substitute for cookies, especially when topped with warm maple syrup.

6 6-inch pancakes

2   tablespoons raisins
2   tablespoons boiling water

1   cup OATMEAL PANCAKE MIX (page 182)
3/4   cup skim milk
1   tablespoon molasses
1   whole egg, beaten (or 1/4 cup egg substitute, thawed)
1   tablespoon canola oil
1   teaspoon cinnamon
Vegetable cooking spray (6 3-second sprays)

Place raisins in boiling water; allow to soften for a minute, then drain off the water. In medium bowl, mix drained raisins with pancake mix and remaining ingredients. Stir just until blended.

Coat nonstick skillet with vegetable cooking spray, and heat. Spoon batter into skillet and cook until browned on both sides.

Nutrient Analysis: 1 pancake
131 Calories, 4 g Fat, 5 g Protein, 19 g Carbohydrate, 191 mg Sodium, 41 mg Cholesterol,
1 g Sat Fat.
Exchanges: 1 fruit, 1 bread.

APPLE OAT PANCAKES

These pleasing pancakes with grated apple and apple juice will be the "apple" of your eye!

6 6-inch pancakes

1   cup OATMEAL PANCAKE MIX (page 182)
1 1/4 cups peeled, grated apple
3/4   cup apple juice
1/4   cup egg substitute, thawed
1   tablespoon canola oil
Vegetable cooking spray (6 3-second sprays)

Combine first 5 ingredients together just until moistened.

Heat a 10-inch non-stick skillet that has been coated with vegetable cooking spray. Cook pancakes until golden brown on both sides. Top with sliced fresh fruit and lowfat yogurt if desired.

Nutrient Analysis: 1 pancake
127 Calories, 3 g Fat, 4 g Protein, 20 g Carbohydrate, 181 mg Sodium, 0 mg Cholesterol,
0 g Sat Fat.
Exchanges: 1/2 fruit, 1 bread, 1/2 fat.

Too much of a good thing can be wonderful!

Mae West

SOUR CREAM PANCAKES

These taste quite a bit like sourdough pancakes.

6 6-inch pancakes

1	cup OATMEAL PANCAKE MIX (page 182)
1	cup lowfat buttermilk
3	tablespoons light sour cream
1	egg white

Vegetable cooking spray (6 3-second sprays)

Combine first four ingredients together just until moistened.

Heat 10 inch non-stick skillet that has been coated with vegetable cooking spray. Cook pancakes on both sides until golden brown.

Serve topped with fresh fruit and VANILLA MAPLE CREAM SYRUP (page 108), if desired.

Nutrient Analysis: 1 pancake (plain)
105 Calories, 2 g Fat, 5 g Protein, 17 g Carbohydrate, 218 mg Sodium, 3 mg Cholesterol,
1 g Sat Fat.
Exchanges: 1 fruit, 1 bread.

COCOA PANCAKES

This is sure to be a hit with chocoholics. The melted mini morsels in each pancake are an unexpected reward for such a low-fat dish.

6 6-inch pancakes

1	cup OATMEAL PANCAKE MIX (page 182)
1	tablespoon + 1 teaspoon cocoa powder
6	tablespoons sugar
3	tablespoons semisweet mini chocolate chips
2	egg whites or 1/4 cup egg substitute, thawed
1	tablespoon canola oil
3/4	cup skim milk

Vegetable cooking spray (6 3-second sprays)
Sifted powdered sugar, optional
Coffee-flavored lowfat yogurt, optional

Combine pancake mix, cocoa, sugar, and chocolate chips, mixing well. Add egg whites, oil, and skim milk, mixing until ingredients are just moistened.

Cook batter in heated nonstick skillet coated with vegetable cooking spray until browned on both sides. Top with sifted powdered sugar and a tablespoon of coffee-flavored lowfat yogurt if desired.

Nutrient Analysis: 1 pancake (plain)
186 Calories, 5 g Fat, 5 g Protein, 30 g Carbohydrate, 194 mg Sodium, 2 mg Cholesterol,
1 g Sat Fat.
Exchanges: 1 fruit, 1 bread, 1 fat.

OVEN PUFFED PANCAKE WITH APPLE FILLING

Those devilishly high fat "Dutch Baby" pancakes can't hold a candle to this delicious low-fat version. With milk and juice, "pro-carbing" was never so easy!

Serves 2

1/4	cup egg substitute, thawed
1	whole egg, beaten
1/3	cup skim milk
1/4	teaspoon real vanilla extract
1/3	cup flour
1/4	teaspoon cinnamon
1	teaspoon sugar
1	teaspoon light stick margarine
1	teaspoon powdered sugar
1/2	cup unsweetened applesauce

Preheat oven to 425° F. Mix first 7 ingredients together with wire whisk until smooth. Let stand for five minutes. Place margarine in 8-inch cast iron skillet and melt in oven until bubbly. Pour pancake batter into skillet. Place back in oven and bake 15-20 minutes until pancake is puffy and golden brown. Remove from oven and top with powdered sugar and applesauce.

Nutrient Analysis: 1 serving
180 Calories, 4 g Fat, 9 g Protein, 26 g Carbohydrate, 120 mg Sodium, 110 mg Cholesterol,
1 g Sat Fat.
Exchanges: 1 fruit, 1 bread, 1 meat.

CHEESY POTATO PANCAKES

4 pancakes

1   cup grated potatoes
2   tablespoons egg substitute, thawed
1/3 cup shredded light cheddar cheese
1   tablespoon grated raw onion
2   teaspoons unbleached flour
Vegetable cooking spray (6 3-second sprays)

Working quickly, squeeze out excess liquid from potatoes.

In small bowl, combine all ingredients. Coat nonstick skillet with cooking spray and heat. Allowing 1/4 cup of mixture for each pancake, cook until light brown, turning once (approximately 5-7 minutes per side). Season with a touch of salt, pepper, or butter substitute like Butter Buds® or Molly McButter®.

Nutrient Analysis: 1 pancake
86 Calories, 3 g Fat, 4 g Protein, 10 g Carbohydrate, 88 mg Sodium, 7 mg Cholesterol,
1 g Sat Fat.
Exchanges: 1 bread.

Nature, time and patience
are the three great physicians.

H. G. Bohn

ALL-IN-ONE PANCAKES

So named because they include a host of nutrient-packed ingredients which provide you with vitamin A, B-vitamins, and protein.

12 pancakes

1	cup whole wheat flour
1	cup unbleached white flour
1/4	cup egg substitute, thawed
2	tablespoons brown sugar
1	teaspoon salt
2	cups skim milk
1/2	cup water
1	large carrot, scraped and diced small
1	cup green onion, thinly sliced
3	celery stalks, diced
1/2	cup water chestnuts, diced
1	cup bean sprouts
1	cup leftover cooked lean meat or fish, diced

Vegetable cooking spray (6 3-second sprays)

Combine flours and the next five ingredients to form thin batter. Fold in vegetables and meat. Pour 1/2 cup batter into 350° F. electric skillet coated with vegetable cooking spray (one 3-second spray for every 2 pancakes). Cook until lightly browned on both sides. Repeat until batter is used up. Serve with low sodium soy sauce.

Nutrient Analysis: 1 pancake (prepared with chicken breast)
131 Calories, 1 g Fat, 8 g Protein, 21 g Carbohydrate, 3 g Fiber, 244 mg Sodium, 13 mg Cholesterol,
0 g Sat Fat.
Exchanges: 1 vegetable, 1 bread, 1/2 meat.
Note: Analysis does not take into account the 200 mg of sodium in each teaspoon of low sodium soy sauce.

MIXED GRAIN WAFFLES

Vanilla yogurt mixed with chopped fresh fruit of your choice makes a colorful and tasty topping.

8 4-inch waffles

1	cup OATMEAL PANCAKE MIX (page 182)
3/4	cup lowfat plain yogurt
1/2	cup 1% milk
1	tablespoon canola oil
2	egg whites, beaten until stiff

Vegetable cooking spray (4 3-second sprays)

Mix pancake mix, yogurt, milk, and oil together; fold in beaten egg whites. Coat nonstick waffle iron with cooking spray. Pour waffle batter into iron; cook according to waffle iron manufacturer's directions.

Nutrient Analysis: 1 waffle
92 Calories, 3 g Fat, 4 g Protein, 12 g Carbohydrate, 146 mg Sodium, 2 mg Cholesterol,
1 g Sat Fat.
Exchanges: 1 bread.

MORNING BLT

A lunch favorite made to order for breakfast.

Serves 1

2   slices turkey bacon
2   slices whole wheat bread
2   teaspoons fat-free mayonnaise or salad dressing
2   slices tomato
2   pieces lettuce or fresh spinach

Fry bacon, draining off excess fat and pat dry. Toast bread, and assemble sandwich, placing turkey bacon on sandwich first.

Nutrient Analysis: 1 serving
206 Calories, 8 g Fat, 10 g Protein, 27 g Carbohydrate, 3 g Fiber, 712 mg Sodium, 31 mg Cholesterol,
2 g Sat Fat.
Exchanges: 1 bread, 1 meat, 1 fat

Variation: Omit 1 slice of turkey bacon and add 2 ounces of roasted chicken or turkey breast and create a "T-BLT" which is a "pro-carb" blockbuster! To be sodium conscious, avoid the prepackaged, processed, luncheon meat turkey or chicken.

Serves 1

Nutrient Analysis: 1 serving
255 Calories, 6 g fat, 20 g Protein, 27 g Carbohydrate, 437 mg Sodium, 86 mg Cholesterol,
1 g Sat Fat.
Exchanges: 1/2 vegetable, 2 bread, 2 meat, 1/2 fat.

PEEK-A-BOO-TOAST

This is one of Donna's favorite ways to cook eggs. She saw it first in the movie "Moonstruck," fried with lots of butter. This is her version.

Serves 1

1   **thick slice whole grain bread (preferably 1/2-inch thick)**
2   **teaspoons light stick margarine**
1   **whole egg**

Heat nonstick skillet. Cut a 1 1/2-inch hole in center of bread slice. Spread both sides with margarine. Place bread in skillet over low heat, turning to lightly brown both sides. Crack egg into bread hole; cook until set. (Don't turn bread over--the egg will cook just fine.)

Nutrient Analysis: 1 serving
225 Calories, 12 g Fat, 10 g Protein, 19 g Carbohydrate, 3 g Fiber, 320 mg Sodium, 213 mg Cholesterol,
4 g Sat Fat.
Exchanges: 1 bread, 1 meat, 2 fat.

That he may be healthy, happy and wise
let him rise early.

John Clarke

FRENCH-STYLE GRILLED CHEESE SANDWICH

A very tasty twist to the conventional grilled cheese approach.If you wish to reduce the total fat and salt still further, use only half the amount of cheese.

Serves 1

2   slices day old white bread
1/4   cup egg substitute, thawed
1/2   cup skim milk

Vegetable cooking spray (1 3-second spray)
1/4   cup (1 ounce) light cheddar cheese, shredded
1/4   cup (1 ounce) light Swiss cheese, shredded

Dip bread slices in a mixture of egg substitute and milk.

Coat nonstick skillet with cooking spray. Cook both sides of bread until golden brown. Top one slice of bread with a mixture of the two cheeses. Place the other slice of bread on top. Continue cooking until cheeses melt (about 10 seconds).

Nutrient Analysis: 1 serving (using cheeses with 3 grams fat per ounce)
365 Calories, 10 g Fat, 33 g Protein, 35 g Carbohydrate, 836 mg Sodium, 43 mg Cholesterol,
5 g Sat Fat.
Exchanges: 4 bread, 2 meat.

CANADIAN BACON BREAD

Thaw the frozen bread dough by placing it in the refrigerator the night before.

2 loaves, 8 slices per loaf

1   loaf whole wheat, frozen bread dough, thawed

1/4   cup egg substitute, thawed
3/4   cup shredded part skim mozzarella cheese
1/4   cup grated Parmesan cheese
1   package (6-ounces) sliced Canadian bacon
Vegetable cooking spray (2 3-second sprays)

Divide thawed bread dough into two portions. Roll out each portion into a 10-inch x 10-inch square.

In small bowl, mix together egg substitute and cheeses. Spread mixture over each dough portion, leaving a two inch border around all edges. Cut sliced Canadian bacon into 1/4 inch strips. Lay strips on top of cheese mixture.

Roll each dough portion jelly-roll fashion. Place seam side down on cooking sheet coated with vegetable cooking spray. Bake at 350° F. for 25 minutes or until golden brown. Cut into slices and serve warm.

Serving suggestion: To reheat, toast slices under broiler until cheese is bubbly.

Nutrient Analysis: 1 slice
115 Calories, 3 g Fat, 9 g Protein, 11 g Carbohydrate, 381 mg Sodium, 19 mg Cholesterol,
1 g Sat Fat.
Exchanges: 1 bread, 1 meat.

EGG STUFFED POTATOES

For fast prep, bake an extra potato or two the night before.

Serves 1

1   **medium potato**
1/2   **cup egg substitute, thawed**
1   **teaspoon light tub margarine**
2   **tablespoons chopped onion**
2   **teaspoons imitation bacon bits**
Picante sauce, optional

Microwave potato on high for 5-7 minutes. Cool and scoop out potato, leaving a 1/4-inch of skin. Set aside, reserving scooped out potato. Crisp the skin in 325° F. oven for 10-15 minutes.

Scramble egg substitute, margarine, chopped onion, and bacon bits in a nonstick skillet until set.   Mix with reserved potato and stuff the shell. Reheat if needed. Serve with picante sauce for extra zip!

Nutrient Analysis: 1 serving (without picante sauce)
300 Calories, 2 g Fat, 14 g Protein, 54 g Carbohydrate, 5 g Fiber (3 g if potato skin is not eaten),
270 mg Sodium, 2 mg Cholesterol,
1 g Sat Fat.
Exchanges: 2 bread, 2 meat, 1/2 fat.

EGG AND CHORIZO IN POTATO SKINS

Serves 1

1   **medium potato**
1/4   **cup egg substitute, thawed**
1/2   **cup TURKEY CHORIZO (page 186)**
1   **teaspoon light tub margarine**

Microwave potato on high for 5-7 minutes. Cool and scoop out potato, leaving a 1/4-inch of skin. Reserve scooped out potato. Crisp the skin in 325°F. oven for 10-15 minutes.

Scramble egg substitute, chorizo, and margarine in nonstick skillet until set. Mix with reserved potato and stuff the shell. Reheat if needed.

Serving Suggestion: Top with 1 tablespoon fat-free or light sour cream and picante sauce for a real treat (neither included in analysis).

Nutrient Analysis: 1 serving
387 Calories, 8 g Fat, 31 g Protein, 54 g Carbohydrate, 5 g Fiber (3 g if potato skin is not eaten),
199 mg Sodium, 65 mg Cholesterol,
2 g Sat Fat.
Exchanges: 2 1/2 bread, 3 meat, 1/2 fat.

ROSTI

Pronounced "Rosh-Tee." A ubiquitous side dish from Switzerland to serve in place of hash browns.

Serves 1

1   medium potato, peeled, shredded, and rinsed in cold water
1   teaspoon canola oil
Vegetable cooking spray (2 3-second sprays)
1   tablespoon chopped green onions (optional)

Place shredded potato into terrycloth towel and squeeze out excess water. Heat oil in 10-inch nonstick skillet. Place potato in skillet, pressing down until it covers the bottom of the pan. Coat uncooked side with vegetable cooking spray. Cook until well-browned on first side, about 5 minutes.

Before turning to brown second side, place a dinner-size plate over the skillet, then invert rosti onto the plate. Slide rosti, uncooked side down, back into the skillet and cook another 5 minutes or until well-browned. Top with green onions and serve.

Nutrient Analysis: 1 serving
202 Calories, 6 g Fat, 2 g Protein, 34 g Carbohydrate, 3 g Fiber, 8 mg Sodium, 0 mg Cholesterol,
0 g Sat Fat.
Exchanges: 2 1/2 bread, 1 fat.

CHEESY POTATO OMELET

Serves 2

1/4	cup evaporated skim milk
1 1/2	cups egg substitute, thawed
2	teaspoons light tub margarine
1	cup leftover peeled and chopped baked potatoes (warmed in microwave for 30 seconds on high)
6	tablespoons shredded light cheese (either Cheddar or Colby)

Mix together evaporated milk and egg substitute in a small bowl. Melt margarine in nonstick skillet and pour in egg substitute mixture. Allow to set slightly, then add potato and shredded cheese. With spatula, fold half of egg mixture onto other side, cooking until cheese is melted.

Serving Suggestion: A fun way to serve brunch at home is to make omelets to order for your guests. Use the cheese-potato omelet as your base recipe and have fillings on hand like TURKEY CHORIZO (page 186), assorted vegetables (mushrooms, bell pepper, onions, broccoli, corn, spinach, chives, chopped tomatoes, etc.) light mayonnaise, and picante sauce. Let creative minds wander!

Nutrient Analysis: 1 serving (with cheese and potato only)
253 Calories, 6 g Fat, 24 g Protein, 24 g Carbohydrate, 457 mg Sodium, 15 mg Cholesterol,
2 g Sat Fat.
Exchanges: 2 bread, 2 meat.

HUEVOS RANCHEROS

Translated, this means ranch-style eggs with beans and a spicy tomato sauce.

Serves 4

Vegetable cooking spray (2 3-second sprays)
4   **corn tortillas**
4   **whole eggs**
2   **cups LOW SODIUM PICANTE SAUCE (page 190)**
2   **cups canned nonfat refried beans, heated**

Place medium-sized skillet over medium heat. Spray with vegetable cooking spray.

Place corn tortillas in skillet and heat each side until lightly browned and crispy. Remove from pan and place each tortilla on serving plate. Coat skillet with vegetable cooking spray and cook eggs to medium done. Place eggs on tortillas, then top each egg with 1/2 cup picante sauce. Serve 1/2 cup refried beans on the side for each serving.

Nutrient Analysis: 1 serving
328 Calories, 8 g Fat, 17 g Protein, 44 g Carbohydrate, 290 mg Sodium, 213 mg Cholesterol,
2 g Sat Fat.
Exchanges: 1 vegetable, 2 1/2 bread, 2 meat.

SUNRISE CARBONARA

A filling combo that answers the question, "What can I do with last night's spaghetti?".
Virtually any pasta will do, but the shorter varieties (macaroni, penne, ziti) are easier to
toss.

Serves 4

2   teaspoons olive oil
4   cups leftover cooked pasta
2   whole eggs, beaten
4   slices turkey bacon, cooked and crumbled
2   tablespoons grated Parmesan cheese
1   green onion, chopped
Fresh chopped parsley for garnish

Heat olive oil in 10-inch skillet over low heat. Add pasta, eggs, turkey bacon, and cheese;
toss until well-mixed and heated through (about 5 minutes). Garnish with green onion and
parsley. Serve.

Nutrient Analysis: 1 serving
255 Calories, 9 g Fat, 11 g Protein, 33 g Carbohydrate, 295 mg Sodium, 18 mg Cholesterol,
2 g Sat Fat.
Exchanges: 2 bread, 1 meat, 1 fat.

Happiness lies, first of all, in health.

G. W. Curtis

CASSEROLE DE LA CASA

A real party pleaser come brunch time!

Serves 4

1   teaspoon canola oil
1/2   cup chopped onion
1/3   cup chopped green pepper

1   teaspoon chili powder
3   tablespoons parsley
2   cloves garlic, chopped
1   medium tomato, seeded and chopped

1/2   pan leftover **LIGHT CORNBREAD** (page 150), crumbled
1   cup cooked **TURKEY CHORIZO** (page 186)
3/4   cup egg substitute, thawed
Vegetable cooking spray (1 3-second spray)

Place oil in nonstick skillet on medium heat, then add onions and peppers. Saute until clear. Add next 4 ingredients, cooking no more than 2-3 minutes. In medium size bowl, combine vegetable mixture with cornbread and chorizo. Mix until all ingredients are well blended and place in 2-quart casserole dish coated with cooking spray. Pour egg substitute evenly on top. Bake in 325° F. oven for 20-25 minutes or until a knife inserted in the center comes out clean.

Nutrient Analysis: 1 serving
207 Calories, 9 g Fat, 19 g Protein, 15 g Carbohydrate, 204 mg Sodium, 55 mg Cholesterol,
0 g Sat Fat.
Exchanges: 1/2 vegetable, 1 bread, 2 meat.

ITALIAN VEGGIE FRITTATA

A frittata is a cross between an omelet and a pancake. A filling breakfast entree or side dish, it's great for a Sunday brunch with toast, fruit, and skim milk. This recipe also provides two daily vegetable servings.

2 servings

1/2	cup chopped onion
1/2	cup chopped bell pepper
1	cup sliced zucchini squash, raw
1	cup sliced yellow squash, raw
1	tablespoon fresh basil, chopped (or 1/2 tsp dried)
2	garlic cloves, minced
4	teaspoons canola oil
1/2	cup low-salt tomato sauce
1	cup egg substitute
3	tablespoons dry bread crumbs

Saute vegetables, basil, and garlic with canola oil in 10-inch cast iron skillet until tender.

Combine tomato sauce and egg substitute in bowl; pour into skillet; cook until partially set. Do not attempt to blend egg mixture. Sprinkle with bread crumbs. Place skillet under broiler and brown 2-3 minutes or until egg is completely set. Serve with a crusty French or Italian bread.

Nutrient Analysis: 1 serving
219 Calories, 9 g Fat, 14 g Protein, 19 g Carbohydrate, 4 g Fiber, 252 mg Sodium, 0 mg Cholesterol,
1 g Sat Fat.
Exchanges: 2 vegetable, 2 meat, 1 fat.

A LIGHTER EGGS BENEDICT

To keep the fat percentage closer to 30%, allow one egg per serving. Use reduced-salt ham and white or wheat toast to reduce sodium.

Serves 4

1/4   **cup vinegar**
4   **whole eggs**
6   **cups water**

8   **slices Canadian bacon**
4   **English muffins, split and toasted (2 halves per serving)**
1 1/2 **cups YOGANDAISE SAUCE (page 191)**

Place vinegar in 2-quart saucepan that is 2/3 full of water. Bring to a slight boil. Crack one egg in a small saucer, and add to water. Repeat with remaining eggs. Cook approximately 5 minutes, or until white is set and yolk is still soft. Heat can be reduced, and eggs can sit an additional 5 minutes before yolks become hard.

In nonstick skillet, lightly fry Canadian bacon until heated through. Place on muffin halves. Remove eggs with slotted spoon and place each on a muffin half. Top each with 6 tablespoons of YOGANDAISE SAUCE.

Nutrient Analysis: 1 serving (with sauce)
402 Calories, 13 g Fat, 39 g Carbohydrate, 32 g Protein, 1216 mg Sodium, 280 mg Cholesterol, 4 g Sat Fat.
Exchanges: 1/2 milk, 2 bread, 3 meat, 1 fat.

STEAK AND EGG FRIED RICE

A deliciously lighter fried rice for brunch time or anytime. Cholesterol watchers can use egg substitute instead of whole eggs.

Serves 2

6   ounces lean chuck steak, raw and minced
Vegetable cooking spray (2 3-second sprays)

2   teaspoons chopped garlic
1/2 cup green onion, thinly sliced
1   teaspoon canola oil
2   cups leftover cooked white rice
2   whole eggs (or 1/2 cup egg substitute, thawed)
Black pepper, freshly ground
Low sodium soy sauce (optional)

Preheat nonstick skillet over medium-high heat. When very hot, add chuck steak and spray with vegetable cooking spray. Continue cooking until meat is just browned. Remove beef from pan. Reduce heat to medium. Saute garlic and green onion in canola oil for 1 - 2 minutes. Add rice, and continue to saute until the rice grains start to lose moisture. Add beef to the rice mixture. Push rice mixture to sides of pan until there is an empty space in the middle of the pan. Lightly beat eggs and scramble them in the empty space of the pan until eggs are set, but still slightly wet. Fold eggs into rice mixture and season with black pepper. Serve with low sodium soy sauce if desired.

Nutrient Analysis: 1 serving (made with whole eggs, no soy sauce)
365 Calories, 13 g Fat, 21 g Protein, 38 g Carbohydrate, 96 mg Sodium, 300 mg Cholesterol,
5 g Sat Fat.
Exchanges: 1/2 vegetable, 2 bread, 2 1/2 meat, 1 fat.

CHEESY GRITS CASSEROLE

You may want to include this dish in your next brunch menu. We modified the traditional higher-fat grits casserole with reduced fat cheese and egg substitute. For a complete meal with "pro-carb connections," serve with a dry toasted English muffin, 1 cup skim milk, and a fresh apple. Low sodium, light cheese can also be used to help decrease the sodium content.

5 cups; 10 servings

3   cups water
1/4   teaspoon salt
3/4   cup quick grits (not instant)

1/4   cup egg substitute, thawed
1   cup shredded light cheddar cheese (preferably 3 grams fat per ounce or less)
1/8   teaspoon garlic powder
3-4   drops Tabasco sauce
1/3   cup chopped green onion
Vegetable cooking spray (1 3-second spray)

Bring water and salt to boil in medium saucepan. Add grits; bring back to a boil and cook 5 minutes, uncovered. Remove from heat.

Stir in remaining ingredients. Pour into 1 1/2 quart casserole dish (coated with cooking spray). Bake in 350° F. oven for 20 minutes until knife inserted comes out clean.

Nutrient analysis: 1 serving
101 Calories, 3 g Fat, 5 g Protein, 12 g Carbohydrate, 268 mg Sodium, 23 mg Cholesterol,
1 g Sat Fat.
Exchanges: 1 bread, 1/2 meat.

COUNTRY FRIED STEAK WITH CREAM GRAVY

A serving of this dish offers more meat (4 ounces) than is recommended for a breakfast portion. Balance your fat and cholesterol intake the rest of the day. For best results, cook only two steaks at a time.

Serves 4

GRAVY:
1	cup skim milk
2	tablespoons flour
2	tablespoons light sour cream
1/2	teaspoon salt
1/4	teaspoon pepper

STEAK:
1	pound round steak, raw, cut 1/2-inch thick
1/2	cup egg substitute, thawed
1	cup flour
2	teaspoons canola oil

Vegetable cooking spray (8 3-second sprays)

In a large saucepan, mix milk and flour together with wire whisk until blended. Bring to a boil over low heat until mixture is thick and bubbly. Remove from heat. Blend in sour cream using wire whisk. Add salt and pepper to taste. Set aside to serve with steak. Can be reheated in microwave oven for 15-30 seconds on high.

Tenderize steak on each side with meat mallet (4-5 seconds per side), and cut into 4 4-ounce portions. Dip each steak into egg substitute, then dredge in flour until fully coated. Place nonstick skillet over medium heat; add 1 teaspoon canola oil and spread around the skillet with a pastry brush. Spray one side of each steak with vegetable cooking spray (one 3-second spray per side), then cook until well-browned. Before turning, spray uncooked side with vegetable cooking spray. Turn steaks, and cook again until well-browned. Serve with 1/4 cup plus 1 tablespoon gravy.

Nutrient Analysis: 1 serving (4 ounce steak with gravy)
321 Calories, 9 g Fat, 32 g Protein, 28 g Carbohydrate, 390 mg Sodium, 95 mg Cholesterol,
3 g Sat Fat.
Exchanges: 2 bread, 3 meat, 1/2 fat.

Do Ahead & Worth the Effort Recipes

*All happiness depends
on a leisurely breakfast*

John Gunther

Do Ahead And Worth The Effort Recipes

ORANGE CAPPUCINO COFFEE MIX

Serves 8

1/2   cup instant coffee powder
1/4   cup light powdered creamer
1/4   cup sugar
1   teaspoon dried orange peel

Mix ingredients together. Store in airtight container.

To serve, add 2 heaping teaspoons to 1 cup boiling water.

Nutrient Analysis: 1 serving
42 Calories, 1 g Fat, 1 g Protein, 10 g Carbohydrate, 2 mg Sodium, 0 mg Cholesterol,
1 g Sat Fat.
Exchanges: 1 fruit.

See Appendix H (page 258) for a discussion of Coffee, Caffeine and Creamers.

As a rough guideline, caffeine intake should be
no more than twice your body weight in milligrams.
If you weigh 130 pounds, have no more
than 260 mg per day.

CAFE AU LAIT MIX

A smooth, mellow and enjoyable drink. Pictured on the front cover of this book!

Serves 16

3/4   **cup light powdered creamer**
3/4   **cup nonfat dry milk powder**
1/3   **cup instant coffee granules**
1/4   **cup light brown sugar**

Mix ingredients together and store in airtight container. To serve, add 2 tablespoons to a cup of boiling water.

Nutrient Analysis: 1 serving
47 Calories, 1 g Fat, 2 g Protein, 9 g Carbohydrate, 31 mg Sodium, 1 mg Cholesterol,
1 g Sat Fat.
Exchanges: 1 fruit.

MEXICAN HOT COCOA MIX

A cocoa mix to be added to milk, not water.

Serves 12

1/2   **cup cocoa powder**
1   **cup granulated sugar**
1/2   **teaspoon salt**

2   **teaspoons cinnamon**
1   **tablespoon light non-dairy whipped topping**

Mix ingredients together (except whipped topping) and place in jar. To serve, mix 1 heaping tablespoon with 1 cup skim milk. Microwave 1 1/2 minutes on high. Stir again to blend.

Serving Suggestion: swirl with a cinnamon stick and top with the light non-dairy whipped topping.

Nutrient Analysis: 1 serving (with whipped topping)
172 Calories, 2 g Fat, 10 g Protein, 19 g Carbohydrate, 216 mg Sodium, 4 mg Cholesterol,
0 g Sat Fat
Exchanges: 1 milk.

Seeing is deceiving. It's eating that's believing.

James Thurber

BAKING MIXES

Note: If you are on a strict low sodium diet, use low sodium baking powder instead of its regular double acting counterpart, and omit the salt. The sodium content of either a pancake, muffin, or biscuit will drop significantly.

OATMEAL PANCAKE MIX

A blend of flours gives this pancake mix its unique flavor. The oats are ground in blender or food processor to produce an oat flour. Because this can be made ahead of time, no one need ever know how easy these pancakes are to prepare.

6 cups of mix

2   cups uncooked rolled oats
2   cups unbleached white flour
2   cups whole wheat flour
2   tablespoons baking powder
4   tablespoons sugar
1 1/2 teaspoons salt

Place oatmeal in food processor with metal blade; process until the oatmeal is the consistency of flour. Mix oat flour with other ingredients and store in airtight container. Shelf life is three months.

Refer to recipes using this mix for nutritional analysis. Look in "Quick Recipes" Section for the following pancake recipes: OATMEAL RAISIN, APPLE OAT, SOUR CREAM, COCOA and MIXED GRAIN WAFFLES.

LIGHT MUFFIN MIX

Most people enjoy muffins, but many store-bought mixes are high in fat. This homemade version is convenient because it can be made ahead of time, and has a shelf-life of three months.

6 cups of mix

3	cups unbleached white flour
3	cups whole wheat flour
6	tablespoons sugar
2	tablespoons + 2 teaspoons baking powder
1 1/2	teaspoons salt

In a large bowl, mix all ingredients together. (A wire whisk or fork evenly distributes the ingredients.) Store in an airtight container for up to three months.

Refer to recipes using this mix for nutritional analysis. Look in "Quick Recipes" Section for the following muffin recipes: "BY DAWN'S EARLY LIGHT," BANANA, PUMPKIN, LEMON PECAN, and BROCCOLI CHEESE.

LIGHT BISCUIT MIX

Having a biscuit mix in your kitchen can be a lifesaver! The regular boxed variety, unfortunately, is high in both total and saturated fat. This recipe has less fat and uses an unsaturated margarine. Once the mix is prepared, store in an airtight container in the refrigerator and it will stay fresh for up to four weeks.

6 1/2 cups mix

6   **cups unbleached white flour**
3   **tablespoons baking powder**
1 1/2 **teaspoons salt**
2/3   **cup unsalted stick margarine**

In a large bowl with a wire whisk, mix together flour, baking powder, and salt. Cut in margarine with pastry blender until crumbly. Store in refrigerator for up to four weeks.

Refer to recipes using this mix for nutrient analysis. Look in "Quick Recipes" Section for FLUFFY BISCUITS and SPEEDY CHEDDAR BISCUITS which use this mix.

COUNTRY-STYLE SAUSAGE

Ask the butcher to grind the pork loin.

12 patties , 1 ounce each

1/2 pound lean pork loin, ground
1/2 pound raw, ground turkey
1 teaspoon black pepper
1/2 teaspoon red pepper
1 teaspoon garlic powder
1 teaspoon onion powder
1 teaspoon basil
1 teaspoon dry mustard
1 teaspoon sugar
1/2 teaspoon sage
Vegetable cooking spray

Mix all ingredients together in a large bowl except for cooking spray. Shape mixture into 12 patties. Broil patties or fry in a medium nonstick skillet coated with vegetable cooking spray.

Storage Note: Uncooked patties can be frozen in a sealed plastic bag for 2-3 months. Thaw patties overnight in the refrigerator before cooking.

Nutrient Analysis: 1 patty
50 calories, 2 g Fat, 7 g Protein, 1 g Carbohydrate, 16 mg Sodium, 30 mg Cholesterol,
1 g Sat Fat.
Exchanges: 1 meat

TURKEY CHORIZO

Pronounced "CHO-REE-ZO," it is a pork sausage with a "Mexican" seasoning blend (garlic, cumin, oregano, paprika, red pepper). Our ground turkey chorizo cuts the fat and keeps the spices and good taste. Add chorizo to dishes such as omelets, casseroles, or stew.

13 - 14 ounces prepared sausage

1 pound ground turkey, raw
1 teaspoon sugar (or equivalent sugar substitute)
3 medium garlic cloves, chopped
1/4 teaspoon black pepper
1/4 teaspoon red pepper
1/4 teaspoon ground coriander
1/8 teaspoon cumin
1 teaspoon paprika
1/2 teaspoon beef extract (BV® or Kitchen Bouquet®)
1/2 teaspoon light (or reduced sodium) soy sauce
Pinch of allspice and cinnamon
1/2 cup water
1 teaspoon olive oil
4-6 drops liquid smoke

Note in purchasing ground turkey: Some are higher in fat than others because skin and other fat is added during grinding. Be sure to choose one that is low in fat (no more than 3 grams per cooked ounce). We prefer Turkey Store® or Louis Rich® brands in the clear refrigerated package, NOT the roll usually found in the frozen food case which is very high in fat.

Brown turkey and sugar in 10-inch skillet. Add remainder of ingredients and cook over low heat until water evaporates (about 20 minutes).

Storgae Note: This mixture can be refirgerated up to one week. Not recommended for freezing as the mix tends to be dry.

This recipe is recommended as an ingredient in BREAKFAST QUESADILLA, EGG & CHORIZO POTATO SKINS, and CHEESY POTATO OMELET.

Nutrient Analysis: 3 ounces
126 Calories, 5 g Fat, 19 g Protein, 2 g Carbohydrate, 60 mg Sodium, 60 mg Cholesterol,
2 g Sat Fat.
Exchanges: 3 meat.

YOGURT CHEESE

Enjoy yogurt cheese as a spread for toast, bagels, or English muffins. Mix with applesauce, preserves, or maple syrup for added sweetness.

8 ounces nonfat plain yogurt

Place nonfat, plain yogurt in strainer lined with a double thickness of cheesecloth or an appropriately-sized coffee filter. Refrigerate and drain until desired consistency is reached (3-4 hours for soft spread, overnight for a firmer cheese).

Nutrient Analysis: 1 cup yogurt cheese
115 Calories, 0 g Fat, 12 g Protein, 16 g Carbohydrate, 174 mg Sodium, 8 mg Cholesterol,
0 g Sat Fat.
Exchanges: 1 milk.

CRUNCHY PEANUT BUTTER BANANA POPS

A great breakfast treat for kids. One banana pop with a large glass of skim milk makes a "pro-carb" connection.

Serves 2

1	medium banana, peeled
3	tablespoons PEANUT BUTTER CREAM (page 106)
1/4	cup low-fat granola

Cut banana in half. Press a popsicle stick into each banana half. Place peanut butter cream and granola in two separate plates. Roll bananas first in peanut butter cream, then granola. Place bananas on another plate and keep in freezer overnight. Serve the next morning.

Nutrient Analysis: 1 serving
133 Calories, 4 g Fat, 5 g Protein, 24 g Carbohydrate, 81 mg Sodium, 0 mg Cholesterol,
1 g Sat Fat.
Exchanges: 2 fruit.

When asked to name their favorite pig-out food,
many confess to a passion for peanut butter.
Per capita, Americans down 3 pounds
of it every year!

APPLE RAISIN GRANOLA

Regular granola is usually high in fat because of the addition of oil, nuts, and coconut. In this recipe, only a small amount of oil is needed. To "pro-carb connect," eat 1 cup of the granola with 1 1/2 cups skim milk.

4 cups; 8 servings

1   **cup uncooked rolled oats, toasted**
1/2   **cup bran flakes**
1/2   **cup Raisin Nut Bran® cereal**
1/2   **cup Honey Nut Cheerios®**
1/2   **cup raisins**
1/2   **cup dried apples**
2   **tablespoons canola oil**
Butter flavored vegetable cooking spray (2 3-second sprays)

To toast oats, spread evenly on ungreased baking sheet. Bake in 300° F. oven for 5 minutes or until lightly browned.

Mix dry ingredients together until uniformly combined. Drizzle with oil and mix again. Spread evenly on cookie sheet coated with cooking spray. Bake at 400° F. for 5 minutes or until golden brown.

Nutrient Analysis: 1/2 cup mix
143 Calories, 4 g Fat, 3 g Protein, 22 g Carbohydrate, 3 g Fiber, 63 mg Sodium, 0 mg Cholesterol,
0 g Sat Fat.
Exchanges: 1 fruit, 1/2 bread, 1 fat.

LOW SODIUM PICANTE SAUCE

A great accompaniment to any of the baked potato dishes, and the HUEVOS RANCHEROS (page 167).

2 cups; 32 servings

4	medium-ripe tomatoes
4-8	Serrano peppers
1/2	cup water, divided
2	cloves garlic, coarsely chopped
1/2	cup red onion, coarsely chopped
2	tablespoons lemon juice
2	teaspoons Papa Dash® or Mrs. Dash® salt substitute
2	tablespoons chopped cilantro (optional)

Wash tomatoes and peppers well. Place in large microwave safe bowl with 1/4 cup water. Cover with plastic wrap that has several slits cut into it. Microwave on high for 8 minutes, then let cool.

Remove stems from peppers, using gloves to keep hot oils from absorbing into your hands. Core the tomatoes and remove the seeds. Add 1/4 cup water and remaining ingredients to the tomatoes and green peppers. Mix in blender or food processor until smooth. May be served warm or chilled.

Nutrient Analysis: 1 tablespoon
5 Calories, 0 g Fat, 0 g Protein, 1 g Carbohydrate, 2 mg Sodium, 0 mg Cholesterol,
0 g Sat Fat.
Exchanges: Free.

YOGANDAISE SAUCE

As a lighter, delicious substitute for Hollandaise, we recommend it for vegetables, A LIGHTER EGGS BENEDICT (page 171), or any of your favorite egg dishes.

1 1/2 cups; 4 servings

2	tablespoons cornstarch
1 1/2	teaspoons dry mustard
2	tablespoons water
1/4	cup white wine
1	cup lowfat plain yogurt
1	egg yolk
1	tablespoon lemon juice
6-8	drops Tabasco sauce

Yellow food coloring (optional)

Combine cornstarch and dry mustard with water in small bowl; blend until smooth. Set aside.   Heat wine in a large saucepan until just boiling; remove from heat, and add cornstarch/mustard mixture. Blend with wire whisk into a thick paste. Add yogurt, 1/4 cup at a time, then blend in egg yolk, lemon juice, and Tabasco sauce.

Place saucepan over very low heat, stirring constantly with wire whisk. Heat until bubbly and slightly thickened. Add 3-4 drops food coloring if desired. Can be refrigerated, then reheated in microwave oven or double boiler.

Nutrient analysis: 3 ounces (approx. 6 tablespoons)
83 Calories, 3 g Fat, 4 g Protein, 9 g Carbohydrate, 46 mg Sodium, 57 mg Cholesterol,
1 g Sat Fat.
Exchanges: 1 bread.

KOLACHES

12 kolaches

1   loaf frozen white bread dough, thawed
1/2   cup of your favorite pie filling (apple, peach, blueberry, or cherry)
2   tablespoons stick margarine, melted
Powdered sugar

Put dough in greased bowl. Cover and let rise overnight.

Punch dough down and cut into 12 pieces. Place in a 13 x 9 x 2 nonstick baking dish. Cover with moist towel and let rise in warm place for 25 minutes. Make a 1-inch depression in the center of each piece. Place a heaping teaspoon of filling in the depression. Brush the rolls with melted margarine.

Bake in a 375° F. oven for 20 minutes or until golden brown. Sprinkle with powdered sugar before serving.

Nutrient Analysis: 1 serving (with 1 teaspoon powdered sugar)
138 Calories, 4 g Fat, 4 g Protein, 17 g Carbohydrate, 211 mg Sodium, 0 mg Cholesterol,
1 g Sat Fat.
Exchanges: 1 fruit, 1 bread.

BANANA BREAD

If you find banana bread a-peeling, follow the recipe for BANANA MUFFINS (page 143). Pour into greased loaf pan and bake at 350° F. for 45 - 50 minutes. Cool 10 minutes before removing from pan.

1 loaf; 12 slices

Nutrient Analysis: 1 slice
120 Calories, 3 g Fat, 3 g Protein, 22 g Carbohydrate, 176 mg Sodium, 0 mg Cholesterol,
0 g Sat Fat.
Exchanges: 1 fruit, 1 bread.

A WORD ON BREAD MACHINES:

Do you love the taste of home-baked bread, but don't have the time or patience to make it? Bread machines make delicious loaves in no time. Just put the ingredients in and the machine does the rest--mixing, kneading, shaping, timing, and baking. Within 3-4 hours, the bread is ready. The price range is anywhere between $75 - $400, dependent upon how elaborate a purchase you wish to make.

While easy to use, precise ingredient measurement and adherence to machine manufacturer instructions are essential. To supplement your bread machine recipe collection, consider the following publication series: THE BREAD MACHINE COOKBOOKS, I through V by Donna German.

HOMEMADE WHOLE WHEAT BREAD

Most commercial whole wheat bread is made from both whole wheat and white flour. This bread is made entirely with whole wheat flour and has a hearty taste that goes well with any meal. Due to the mixing, rising, and kneading time, it is not quick to prepare. Give it a try when you have extra time on Saturday or Sunday. This recipe yields two loaves, so consider freezing one for later.

2 loaves; 16 slices per loaf

2	cups skim milk
1/2	cup light brown sugar
2	teaspoons salt
1/4	cup stick margarine
1	cup warm water (105 - 115° F.)
2	packages active dry yeast
8	cups unsifted whole wheat flour

Unbleached white flour

In medium saucepan, heat milk until scalding; remove from heat. Add sugar, salt, and margarine; stir until margarine is melted. Cool to lukewarm. Into large mixing bowl, pour warm water. Sprinkle yeast over warm water. Stir to dissolve, (letting stand until yeast is bubbly), then stir in lukewarm milk mixture.

Add 4 cups whole wheat flour; beat until smooth. Gradually add remainder of whole wheat flour, mixing until dough is stiff enough to leave sides of bowl. (This mixing can be done with a spoon if your mixer is not large enough for this task.) Turn dough onto floured surface. Knead about 5 minutes, until dough is smooth and elastic. Place in lightly greased large bowl, turning to coat. Cover with towel and let rise in warm place (80 - 85° F.) until doubled in bulk (about one hour). Punch down dough, and divide into two parts. Shape into loaves and place in greased loaf pans(9 x 5 x 2 3/4). Let rise in warm place until sides come to top of pans (about one hour).

Bake with foil for remainder of baking time. in 375°F. oven for 35-40 minutes. Note: Check after 25 minutes; if crust is very dark, cover The crust will be a deep golden brown when ready.

Nutrient Analysis: 1 slice
126 Calories, 1 g Fat, 5 g Protein, 24 g Carbohydrate, 4 g Fiber, 163 mg Sodium, 0 mg Cholesterol,
0 g Sat Fat.
Exchanges: 1 1/2 bread.

Whole grain breads are high in
complex carbohydrates and low in saturated fats.
Germany has an annual per capita consumption
that is the largest in the world at 154 pounds!
Whole grain bread consumption in the U.S.
stands at 58 pounds per capita.

BAKED FRUIT COMPOTE

The assortment of flavors in this dish blend well into any breakfast. We suggest serving this with the OVEN PUFFED PANCAKE (page 155).

Serves 12

1   can (16-ounces) pitted dark cherries, packed in their own juice,
1/2   cup firmly packed brown sugar
1   tablespoon cornstarch
2 1/2 tablespoons fresh squeezed lemon juice
1/2   cup orange juice

1   can (29-ounces) unsweetened sliced peaches, drained
1   package (6-ounces) dried apricots
1   package (6-ounces) pitted prunes, halved

Drain cherries, reserving 1 cup plus 1 tablespoon juice. Combine brown sugar and cornstarch in medium bowl and gradually add 1 cup cherry juice, lemon juice, and orange juice. Set aside.

Combine peaches, apricots, and prunes in a 2-quart casserole. Pour cornstarch/juice mixture over fruit, then sprinkle with 1 tablespoon cherry juice. Cover and bake in 350° F. oven for 45 - 50 minutes.

Nutrient Analysis: 1 serving
182 Calories, 0 g Fat, 2 g Protein, 47 g Carbohydrate, 3 g Fiber, 19 mg Sodium, 0 mg Cholesterol,
0 g Sat Fat.
Exchanges: 3 fruit.

SWISS OATMEAL

Swiss oatmeal is a hearty mix good to have on hand for those cold winter mornings. Add skim milk and juice for a high energy, low-fat start to your day.

4 cups, 8 servings

1   package (6-ounces) mixed, chopped, dried fruit
1/4   cup wheat germ, toasted
2 1/2 cups uncooked, rolled oats
1/4   cup slivered almonds
1/4   cup shelled, dry-roasted sunflower seeds

Mix all ingredients together. Store in airtight container at room temperature for up to two months.

Preparation for 1 serving: Bring 1 cup water to boil in small saucepan and add 1/2 cup mix. Cook, stirring frequently for 1 minute. Cover and let stand 2 minutes.

Nutrient analysis: 1/2 cup mix
198 Calories, 5 g Fat, 7 g Protein, 32 g Carbohydrate, 6 g Fiber, 4 mg Sodium, 0 mg Cholesterol,
1 g Sat Fat.
Exchanges: 1 fruit, 1 bread, 1 fat.

OATMEAL CUSTARD

This recipe is a modification of a winner of the Quaker Silver Plate recipe contest.
Egg substitute replaces whole eggs, and skim milk keeps saturated fat content low.

Serves 4

2 3/4 cup water
1   cup uncooked rolled oats

1/2   cup egg substitute, thawed
1/4   cup sugar
1 1/3 cups skim milk
1/2   teaspoon vanilla extract
1/8   teaspoon salt
1/3   cup chopped dried fruit (your choice)
1/2   teaspoon cinnamon
Vegetable cooking spray (1 3-second spray)

Boil water in covered saucepan. Stir in oats. Return to a boil, reduce heat and continue to boil. Cook uncovered for about one minute, stirring occasionally. Remove from heat. Cover and set aside.

In large bowl, mix egg substitute, sugar, milk, vanilla, and salt. Add cooked oatmeal, dried fruit and cinnamon to egg mixture and mix well. Pour into 8-inch square pan coated with vegetable cooking spray. Place in larger pan of hot water. Bake in 350° F. oven for one hour or until set.

Serving Suggestion: Top each serving with 1/2 cup sweetened fresh fruit, such as strawberry or peach slices.

Nutrient Analysis: 1 serving
156 Calories, 2 g Fat, 7 g Protein, 30 g Carbohydrate, 3 g Fiber, 90 mg Sodium, 0 mg Cholesterol,
0 g Sat Fat.
Exchanges: 1/2 milk, 1/2 fruit, 1 bread.

WAFFLE CRUNCH CEREAL

A different way to serve waffles.

Serves 4

8 round waffles, frozen
1/8 teaspoon cinnamon and 1 teaspoon sugar
OR
2 tablespoons chopped fresh or dried fruit and 1 tablespoon nuts

Preheat oven to 200° F. Place waffles on ungreased cookie sheet. Toast in the oven for 1 hour, turning waffles after 30 minutes. Let cool. To serve, break 2 waffles into small pieces and place in cereal bowl. Sprinkle with your choice of toppings and pour a cup of skim milk over cereal.

Nutrient Analysis: 4 servings
(2 waffles with skim milk, 2 tablespoons chopped dates,1 tablespoon walnuts per serving)
448 Calories, 15 g Fat, 16 g Protein, 60 g Carbohydrate, 732 mg Sodium, 1 mg Cholesterol,
4 g Sat Fat.
Exchanges: 1 milk, 1 fruit, 2 bread, 3 fat.

BEAT THE "BLUES" COFFEE CAKE

Bake this on Sunday and your first day back to work on Monday will be a little nicer.

Serves 9

SAUCE:
1 1/4 cups fresh or frozen (and thawed) blueberries
1/3   cup sugar
2   tablespoons cornstarch

CAKE:
1   cup all purpose flour
1   cup whole wheat flour
1/4   cup sugar
1/4   teaspoon salt
2   teaspoons baking powder
3   tablespoons light tub margarine, chilled
1   cup skim milk
1   whole egg, lightly beaten
1   teaspoon vanilla extract

GLAZE:
1/2   cup powdered sugar
1 1/2 teaspoons warm water
1/4 teaspoon almond extract

Combine blueberries, sugar and cornstarch in small saucepan. Cook over medium heat, stirring occasionally, for 5 minutes or until sauce is thickened. Set aside.

Mix flours, sugar, salt and baking powder with a fork. Cut in margarine with pastry blender until mixture resembles coarse meal. Add milk, egg and vanilla and mix until dry ingredients are just moistened.

To assemble, pour half of batter into greased 8-inch square pan. Pour half of blueberry sauce over batter. Repeat with remaining batter and sauce. Bake in preheated 375° F. oven for 25 to 35 minutes or until toothpick inserted comes out clean.

Prepare glaze while coffeecake bakes. In small bowl mix together powdered sugar, water and almond extract. Let coffee cake cool for 5-10 minutes before drizzling with glaze.

Nutrient Analysis: 1 serving
210 Calories, 3 g Fat, 3 g Protein, 38 g Carbohydrate, 3 g Fiber, 210 mg Sodium, 24 mg Cholesterol,
1 g Sat Fat.
Exchanges: 2 fruit, 1 bread.

OVEN FRIED POTATOES

Donna's husband, Jeff, came up with this recipe as a substitute for home fries. The preparation time is about 45 minutes. Since this bakes for 30 minutes in a 375°F. oven, use a skillet that can take the heat. He suggests the 10-inch cast iron type.

Serves 3

1 1/2 teaspoons canola oil
3   cups peeled, cubed, uncooked potatoes
Vegetable cooking spray (2 3-second sprays)
1/2   teaspoon dry rosemary, crushed

Preheat oven to 375° F. Heat oil in skillet, then add potatoes. Coat with two sprays of vegetable cooking spray. Stir every minute for about 10 minutes until lightly brown.

Place in preheated oven for 15 minutes. After this time, stir potatoes to redistribute. Add rosemary and bake for another 15 minutes, or until well- browned.

Nutrient Analysis: 1 serving
128 Calories, 3 g Fat, 1 g Protein, 24 g Carbohydrate, 4 g Fiber, 8 mg Sodium, 0 mg Cholesterol, 0 g Sat Fat.
Exchanges: 1 bread, 1 fat.

What I say is that, if a man really likes potatoes,
he must be a pretty decent sort of fellow.

A. A. Milne

BRUNCH BAKE

A tasty alternative to the traditional egg-sausage-cheese bake. Prepare this simple dish the night before, then bring to room temperature before baking.

Serves 8

1	pound loaf day old French bread

Vegetable cooking spray (2 3-second sprays)

1	cup egg substitute, thawed
4	whole eggs
6	tablespoons white wine
1	teaspoon Italian seasoning
6	ounces reduced-salt ham, diced
1/2	cup chopped green onions
1/2	cup shredded part-skim mozzarella cheese

Remove ends from French bread; slice remainder of loaf into 1-inch thick slices. If bread is fresh, place slices in 200° F oven for 10 minutes. Then cool at room temperature for 10 minutes. Coat 13 x 9 x 2 inch baking pan with vegetable cooking spray.

Line pan with bread, cut side down. Beat egg substitute and eggs with wine and Italian seasoning. Pour over bread slices and top with ham, green onions, then cheese. Let sit at least one hour at room temperature or refrigerate overnight. Cover with aluminum foil, and bake in 350° F oven for 20 minutes. Remove foil and continue to bake for another 10 minutes, or until edges of bread start to brown.

Nutrient Analysis: 1 serving
280 Calories, 9 g Fat, 17 g Protein, 30 g Carbohydrate, 626 mg Sodium, 136 mg Cholesterol,
2g Sat Fat.
Exchanges: 2 bread, 2 meat.

BLACKENED TUNA HASH

If fresh tuna is too pricy, substitute snapper, catfish, or cod.

4 servings

1/2	pound raw tuna steaks, cut into 3/4" cubes
2	tablespoons light (or reduced-sodium) soy sauce
1	teaspoon sugar
2	teaspoons canola oil

Vegetable cooking spray (2 3-second sprays)

1/2	cup chopped green onion
1/2	cup chopped red pepper
1/2	cup diced water chestnuts
3/4	cup red onion
1	teaspoon canola oil

Vegetable cooking spray (2 3-second sprays)

1	teaspoon chopped garlic
2	tablespoons chopped parsley
1/2	teaspoon cayenne
1/4	teaspoon black pepper
1/2	teaspoon dried thyme
3	cups OVEN FRIED POTATOES (page 202)

Marinate tuna in soy sauce and sugar for 30 minutes. Remove tuna from marinade and pat dry with paper towel. Place tuna in nonstick skillet containing 2 teaspoons canola oil and vegetable cooking spray. Cook over medium high heat for 3-4 minutes until tuna is darkened, but not burnt, and set aside.

Using electric nonstick skillet, saute green onion, red pepper, water chestnuts and red onion in 1 teaspoon canola oil and vegetable cooking spray until clear. Add next five ingredients and continue to saute for 2-3 minutes.

To serve, combine tuna and potatoes with vegetable mixture in electric skillet and heat through.

Nutrient Analysis: 1 serving
314 Calories, 8 g Fat, 17 g Protein, 42 g Carbohydrate, 5 g Fiber, 332 mg Sodium, 21 mg Cholesterol,
1 g Sat Fat.
Exchanges: 1 vegetable, 2 bread, 2 meat, 1 fat.

A change of heart is the essence
of all other change, and it is brought about
by a re-education of the mind.

Emmeline Pethick-Lawrence

HAM AND CHEESE CALZONE WITH APPLES

"Calzone", which means trouser leg in Italian, is a pizza folded in half like a turnover. If you are reducing sodium, use Oscar Meyer® or Weight Watchers® lower-salt ham. Doing this will drop the sodium content per serving to 375 mg.

Serves 4

1 1/2 teaspoons canola oil
1   cup thinly sliced yellow onion
2/3   pound lean, low salt ham, diced
2   cups peeled, sliced Golden Delicious apples

1/4   cup orange juice
1   tablespoon brown sugar
Freshly ground pepper to taste

2   ounces light cheddar cheese, shredded
1   tube Pillsbury® pizza crust dough, divided into two pieces
1   tablespoon cornmeal

Preheat oven to 375° F. Heat oil in 350° F. electric skillet. Saute onions until clear, then add ham and cook until water from the ham evaporates. Add apples and cook until just tender.

Add orange juice, brown sugar, and black pepper to taste. Cook until orange juice is absorbed. Let cool 10 minutes.

Place half the filling on each piece of dough and top with cheese. Moisten edges with milk or water, then fold over into half-moon shape. Sprinkle cornmeal on baking sheet and place calzones on top of brand cornmeal. Bake 18-20 minutes or until golden brown. Cut each calzone in half and serve.

Nutrient Analysis: 1 serving
410 Calories, 12 g Fat, 22 g Protein, 50 g Carbohydrate, 1076 mg Sodium, 50 mg Cholesterol,
3 g Sat Fat.
Exchanges: 1 vegetable, 1 fruit, 2 bread, 2 meat, 1 fat.

PIZZA RAMEN-EASE OMELET

This is a brunch masterpiece, if we may say so ourselves, and it's featured on the cover of this book! Don't be put off by the fat content. Use only 1/2 the seasoning packet found with the noodles to help cut back on the sodium.

Serves 2

1   package low-fat ramen noodles (any flavor)
2   whole eggs
1/2 cup egg substitute, thawed
1/4 cup chopped green onion
1   teaspoon chives
1   tablespoon chopped parsley
1/4 teaspoon garlic powder
1/8 teaspoon Tabasco sauce

2   tablespoons water
2   teaspoons olive oil
3/4 cup diced tomatoes
1/2 cup fresh sliced mushrooms
1/2 cup shredded light provolone or part-skim mozzarella cheese
Vegetable cooking spray

Prepare ramen noodles according to package directions, but reserve seasoning packet. Preheat oven broiler. Crack eggs into a medium size bowl, then add 1/2 the seasoning packet, egg substitute, green onion, chives, parsley, garlic powder, tabasco sauce, and water. Beat with fork or wire whisk until combined.

Heat olive oil in nonstick skillet over medium heat and add noodles. Distribute noodles so they evenly cover the bottom of the skillet. Reduce heat to low, then pour eggs over noodles. Cook until eggs are no longer wet and nearly set. Slide the "pizza" onto a cookie sheet coated with cooking spray. Top with tomatoes, mushrooms, and cheese, then place under broiler on the middle oven rack so as not to burn the eggs. Remove as soon as cheese melts evenly, and cut into wedges for presentation.

Nutrient Analysis: 1 serving
429 Calories, 17 g Fat, 28 g Protein, 39 g Carbohydrate, 450 mg Sodium, 232 mg Cholesterol,
4 g Sat Fat.
Exchanges: 1 vegetable, 2 bread, 2 1/2 meat, 2 fat.

Ancient folklore purported that when eggs
are eaten upon wakening, a revitalization
of the body and spirit is sure to result.

MEXICAN SCRAMBLE

Experience this Mexican breakfast rendition of eggs, tortilla strips, and other delicacies cooked together. We lightened the load and still came up with a sumptuous dish.

Serves 4

3	6-inch corn tortillas

Vegetable cooking spray (2 3-second sprays)

1	teaspoon olive oil
1/2	cup chopped onion
2	cloves garlic, chopped
2	jalapeno peppers, seeded and chopped
1	small can (8 ounces) whole peeled tomatoes
1/4	teaspoon ground cumin
1/2	teaspoon ground coriander
1/4	teaspoon dried marjoram
1/4	teaspoon dried oregano

Black pepper to taste

3	whole eggs
3/4	cup egg substitute, thawed
3	tablespoons water

Vegetable cooking spray
Cilantro and green onion, chopped (for optional garnish)

TORTILLAS:

Cut each corn tortilla in half, then into 1-inch wide strips. Coat with vegetable cooking spray and bake in 400° F oven 5-8 minutes or until crisp.

SAUCE:

In a 10-inch skillet or Dutch oven, saute the onion in olive oil until onions are translucent. Add the garlic and continue to saute for about a minute. Add the jalapeno peppers and the tomatoes (along with their liquid), turning to simmer. Break up the tomatoes with a wooden or plastic spoon, and continue to simmer for 15-20 minutes or until mixture resembles a chunky sauce. Then add cumin, coriander, marjoram, oregano, and black pepper to taste. Allow to simmer for another 10 minutes for the flavors to blend.

EGGS:

Beat the eggs and egg substitute together with 3 tablespoons water. Coat a nonstick skillet with cooking spray. Add egg mixture and cook just until set.

ASSEMBLY:

Mix in the tortilla strips and cook until eggs are fully set. To serve, divide the egg mixture into four portions. Serve with sauce and sprinkle with cilantro and green onion if desired.

Nutrient Analysis: 1 serving
157 Calories, 6 g Fat, 11 g Protein, 14 g Carbohydrate, 211 mg Sodium, 160 mg Cholesterol,
2 g Sat Fat.
Exchanges: 1 vegetable, 1/2 bread, 2 meat.

SEAFOOD QUICHE

Reserve 1 hour and 15 minutes to prepare this dish. Instead of a fatty, time consuming crust, we used shredded potatoes for a mouth watering effect. If salmon is too expensive, try cod, trout, or haddock.

9-inch pie; 4 servings

QUICHE:

5	ounces fresh salmon steak
5	ounces fresh whitefish (snapper, cod, or whatever white-flesh fish is on sale)
2	fluid ounces white wine, divided
1	very large, peeled Idaho potato
2	teaspoons olive oil
1/4	cup chopped green onion
1/4	cup chopped red onion
2	tablespoons chopped parsley
2	whole eggs, lightly beaten
1/2	cup egg substitute, thawed
2	teaspoons Dijon mustard
6-8	Arugula leaves for garnish

Vegetable cooking spray (2 3-second sprays)

CREAMY MUSTARD SAUCE:

2	tablespoons mustard
4	teaspoons fresh squeezed lemon juice
8	tablespoons plain lowfat yogurt
5-6	drops Tabasco sauce

Steam salmon and whitefish. To do so, place steamer basket in Dutch oven with one inch of water. Cover Dutch oven and put on medium heat until wisps of steam appear. Put a plate large enough to accommodate the fish on top the steamer basket. Place fish on plate and sprinkle with one ounce of white wine. Steam for seven minutes. Remove from steamer, let cool and remove bones and skin from salmon. Break into bite-size pieces. Set aside.

Preheat oven to 425° F. Shred the potato, place in strainer and squeeze out excess moisture. Mix potato with olive oil. Salt and pepper to taste. Pat potato in base and sides of a 9-inch pie pan coated with vegetable cooking spray. Spray potato with nonstick cooking spray. Bake for 20 minutes at 425° F. Remove from oven.

Reset oven temperature to 350° F. Place fish pieces in potato crust. Mix onions and parsley together and place atop the fish. Beat eggs, egg substitute, Dijon mustard, and the other ounce of white wine together until smooth. Pour atop the onions and parsley. Bake for 25 minutes. Cut into 4 wedges.

To prepare Creamy Mustard Sauce, combine sauce ingredients and blend with wire whisk until smooth. Serve fish with sauce.

Nutrient Analysis: 1 serving (with 3 tablespoons sauce)
263 Calories, 11 g Fat, 23 g Protein, 16 g Carbohydrate, 410 mg Sodium, 156 mg Cholesterol,
2 g Sat Fat.
Exchanges: 1 bread, 2 meat, 1 fat.

Shopping Guides & Recipe Modifications

*We often live as if our
habits don't matter. They do.*

John Farquhar

Shopping Guides and Recipe Modifications

SHOPPING GUIDES

Nutrient values found within the shopping guide listings were obtained from two major sources:
1. Manufacturer's information found on the nutrition label
2. Pennington, Jean. FOOD VALUES OF PORTIONS COMMONLY USED, 16th Edition. New York: J.B. Lippincott Company, Inc., 1994.

Foods listed in the Shopping Guides do not constitute an endorsement of those foods or define a particular food as "good" or "bad." The authors have not included registered trademarks on brand name items.

CEREALS
The criteria for cereal selection are as follows:

1. 120 calories or less per serving
2. No more than 3 grams of fat
3. 3 or more grams of fiber
4. At least 25% of the recommended daily intake for iron

The symbol ^ indicates a cereal having a sodium content of 180 milligrams or less per serving) If your favorite cereal is missing from the guide, try mixing it with one of the recommended brands.

Cold Cereal -- Brand Name

A&P
    40% Bran Flakes
    Raisin Bran
ARROWHEAD MILLS
    ^Flake Cereals (all varieties)

BARBARA'S
     ^Raisin Bran
EREWHON
     ^Low Sodium Crispy Brown Rice
     ^Raisin Bran
     ^Wheat Flakes
GENERAL MILLS
     ^Clusters
     ^Fiber One
     ^Raisin Nut Bran
     Wheaties
     Whole Wheat Total
GIANT
     ^Bite Size Shredded Wheat
     40% Bran Flakes
HEALTH VALLEY (found in most major supermarkets)
     ^Amaranth Flakes
     ^Amaranth with Banana
     ^Fat Free Granola
     ^Fiber 7 Flakes
     ^Fruit and Fitness
     ^Fruit and Nut Oat Bran O's
     ^Oat Bran Flakes
     ^Oat Bran Flakes with Almonds and Dates
     ^Oat Bran Flakes with Raisins
     ^Oat Bran O's
     ^100% Natural Bran
     ^Natural Bran with Apples and Cinnamon
     ^Raisin Bran
     ^Sprouts 7 with Raisins
     ^Swiss Breakfast Muesli (Raisin and Nut)
     ^Swiss Breakfast Muesli (Tropical Fruit)
HEALTHY CHOICE

MultiGrain Flakes
^Multi Grain Squares (1 ounce serving)
IGA
Bran Flakes
Raisin Bran
KELLOGGS
All Bran
Apple Raisin Crisp
Bran Flakes
Common Sense Oat Bran
^Cracklin Oat Bran
^Heartwise Flakes
^Heartwise Nuggets
^Low Fat Granola (only 2 grams fiber per serving)
^Mueslix
Nutrigrain (Raisin Bran and Almond Raisin)
Raisin Bran
^Shredded Wheat Squares (Strawberry and Blueberry)
KOLLN
^Fruit and Oat Bran Crunch
^Oat Bran Crunch
KRETCHMER
^Wheat Germ
MALT-O-MEAL
Bran Flakes
Raisin Bran
NABISCO
^Fruit Wheats (Strawberry, Raspberry, Blueberry, and Oat Bran/Raisin)
^Shredded Wheat Biscuit
^Spoon Size Shredded Wheat
^100% Bran
^100% Oat Bran

POST Bran Flakes
    ^Fruit and Fibre (all flavors)
    ^Grape Nuts Flakes
    ^Great Grains (watch portion size!)
    ^Raisin Bran
QUAKER
    Crunchy Corn Bran
    ^Shredded Wheat
    Life (Regular and Cinnamon)
    Low-Fat Granola
    Multi Grain Cereal
    ^Oat Bran
RALSTON
    ^Bran News
    Chex (Multi Bran)
    ^Fruit Muesli (all flavors)
    Multi Bran Chex
    Oat Bran Options
    ^Rice Bran Options
    Sun Flakes
SAFEWAY
    40% Bran Flakes
    Raisin Bran
SKINNER
    ^Raisin Bran
UNCLE SAM
    ^Whole Grain Wheat Flakes
Hot Cereals -- Brand Name
AMERICAN HOME
    Wheatena
ARROWHEAD MILLS
    ^Hot Oat Bran
    ^Instant Oatmeal (Apple, Date, and Almond; and Apple Spice Flavors)

BARBARAS
    ^14 Grains Hot Cereal
HEALTH VALLEY
    ^Oat Bran
KOLLN
    ^Premium Oatmeal
KROGER
    ^Oat Bran
MOTHERS
    ^Whole Wheat and Oat Bran
NABISCO
    ^Instant Oat Bran
    ^Wholesome and Hearty Oat Bran
THREE MINUTE BRAND
    ^Instant Oat Bran
    ^Oat Bran (Regular or Toasted)
    ^Quick Oats and Toasted Oat Bran
    ^Quick Pan Toasted Oats
QUAKER Oat Bran
    ^Quick Malt-O-Meal + Oat Bran
    Quick Oats
RALSTON
    ^High Fiber Oat Cereal

CHEESE

Note: As a general rule, look for cheese with 3 grams of fat or less per ounce and no more than 2 grams of saturated fat. For sodium watchers, choose cheese with 160 milligrams or less per ounce. Lower-sodium cheese is marked with the symbol ^. Recommended types of cheese are given below.

American:
    Borden Fat Free Slices

Healthy Choice Free
Kraft Free Slices

Weight Watchers Fat Free Slices
Borden Lite Line
^Borden Lite Lite Low Sodium
Tasty-Lo
Weight Watchers Slices
^Weight Watchers Low Sodium Slices

Cheddar:
Alpine Lace Free N'Lean
Healthy Choice
Kraft Free
Borden Light Line
Cabot 75% Reduced Fat Cheddar
Weight Watchers Slices
^County Line Advantage
Kraft Healthy Favorites

Colby:
Borden Light Line
^County Line Advantage
^Edam Tasty Lo

Cheese Spreads:
Alpine Lace Spread (all flavors)
^Sargento Pot Cheese
Laughing Cow (labeled in green)
Cost Cutter

White Cheeses: Fat Free, Light, Or Low Fat

Cream Cheese:
> Healthy Choice Free
> Philadelphia Free
> ^Weight Watchers
> ^Mrs. Margareten's Parvemage

Mozzarella:
> Alpine Lace Free and Lean
> Healthy Choice Fat Free
> Healthy Choice Mozzarella & Cheddar
> Polly-O Free
> ^County Line Advantage
> ^Frigo Truly Light
> ^Lifetime Natural
> ^Sargento MooTown Snackers
> ^County Line Light
> ^Sargento Preferred Light
> Polly-O Lite

Ricotta:
> Polly-O Free
> ^Crystal Farm's Lite
> ^Sargento Lite
> ^Frigo Low Fat Low Salt
> ^Frigo Truly Lite
> ^Part Skim (most brands)

Swiss:
> Lifetime
> Borden Light Line
> Weight Watchers Swiss Slices
> ^County Line Advantage (only 8 milligrams sodium)

Muenster:
> Borden Light Line

Monterey Jack:
> Borden Light Line

"Hard-to-Categorize" Cheeses:
> Healthy Choice Mexican
> Borden Light Line Jalapeno
> Tasty-Lo Dill or Garlic
> Tasty-Lo Hot Pepper or Onion

Cottage Cheese: All 1/2 cup servings. By variety with Calories, Fat (g) and Sodium (mg).

Variety	Calories	Fat (g)	Sodium (mg)
Nonfat varieties	70	0 g	420 mg
1% fat varieties	80	1 g	450 mg
2% fat varieties	100	2 g	450 mg
Dry curd varieties	60	less than 1 g	10-20 mg

The selection of hot chocolate mixes is mind-boggling! Table 13 compares some popular brands, ranked in order of fat amounts (highest to lowest). Fat values don't include milk unless indicated.

Table 13: Hot Chocolate Comparisons

Brand	Calories	Fat (g)
Alpine (1 pkt)	150	5
Swiss Miss Regular (1 pkt)	110	3
Carnation Instant (1 pkt)	110	1
Swiss Miss Sugar Free (1 pkt)	50	less than 1
Carnation Instant Sugar Free (1 pkt)	50	less than 1

Carnation Instant Diet (1 pkt)	25	less than 1
Hershey's Cocoa (1 tsp)	120	less than 1
(add 2 tsp. sugar and 1 cup lowfat milk)		
Ovaltine (3/4 ounce)	80	0

COFFEE CAKE, DANISH, AND GRANOLA BARS
American Home Fat-Free Coffee Cake
Entenmann's Danish and Muffins
Hostess Light Twinkies, Cupcakes, and Crumb Cakes
Little Debbie Apple Struesel Coffee Cake
Weight Watchers Cinnamon Rolls and Cheese Sweet Rolls
Any grocery store bakery variety that indicates "low-fat" or "fat free" on the label
Nabisco Snack Wells Fruit Bars

To control fat intake, a few of the crackers have recommended serving sizes in parentheses.

Table 14: Fat-Free and Low-Fat Cracker Choices

FAT-FREE (less than 1 g/serving)	LOW-FAT (1-2 g/serving)
Wasa Golden Rye	Saltines (Food Club) (6)
Wasa Light Rye	Krispy Saltines (Sunshine) (6)
Light Rye Nabisco	Premium Saltines (regular or unsalted, 6)
Kavli Norwegian Crispbread	
Nabisco Snack Wells:	
Wheat and Cracked Pepper have no fat	Snack Wells Classic Golden Reduced Fat (5)
Savoir Faire:	
Fin Crisp/Rye Crisp	Crown Pilot (1)
Cocktail Minitoast	Dandy Soup and Oyster (20)
Biscottes	Royal Lunch (1)
Jacobsen:	Garden Crisps (6)
Cinnamon Snack Toast	Reduced Fat Triscuits (5)

Original
Lavosh
Original Dutch Crisp
RW Frookie

Uneeda Biscuits (3)
Harvest Crisp (all flavors) (6)
Zwieback Toast (2)
Honey Maid Grahams (4 single squares)
Ak Mak Sesame Crackers (2)

Hard Tack
Rice Cakes

Matzos (Maneschewitz)

Quaker Rice Cakes (all flavors)
Quaker Corn Cakes (all flavors)
Quaker Caramel Corn Cakes

Red Oval Farms:
Stoned Corn Crackers (4)
Stoned Rye Crackers (4)
Stoned Wheat Thins (4)

Hol Grain (at select stores):
Brown Rice Lite
Snack Thins
Whole Wheat
Old London Melba Toast
Whole Wheat
Rye

Pepperidge Farm:
Wholesome Choice (all flavors) (6)
Wasa Crispbread (2)
Hain Mini Rice Cakes:
Cheese or Nacho Flavor (5)
Reduced Fat Wheat Thins (5-9)
Barbara's Breadsticks (3)

Old London:
Krisp & Natural Crackerbread (1)
Melba Toast (all flavors)
Fattoria & Pandea Brand Breadsticks (3)

Hain Mini Rice Cakes and
Crispy Cakes (all flavors)

Health Valley Fat Free (all varieties)
Nabisco Fat-Free Saltines

EGG SUBSTITUTES: Some common choices found in freezer section
Fleishmann's Eggbeaters:
    Regular, Cheese, and Vegetable Omelet Mixes
Food Club Egg Substitute
Healthy Choice Egg Substitute
Kroger Egg Substitute
Lyle Farms Natural Choice
Morningstar Farms Better N' Eggs

Table 15: Frozen Breakfast Options

	Cal	Fat (g)	Pro. (g)	Carbo. (g)	Sodium (mg)
Sandwiches:					
Swanson Great Starts Breakfast Burrito (Original)	200	7	8	25	510
Weight Watchers English Muffin Sandwich	230	8	13	25	590
Weight Watchers Ham & Cheese Bagel Sandwich	210	6	13	28	460
Weight Watchers Vegetable Omelet Sandwich	210	6	9	28	330
Weight Watchers Handy Ham & Cheese Omelet	180	5	14	18	420
Weight Watchers Cinnamon Rolls	180	5	4	31	170
Weight Watchers Cheese Sweet Rolls	180	4	5	32	210
Frozen Pancakes:					
Aunt Jemima, Hungry Jack, and others (average values for 3)	230	4	5	45	600
Aunt Jemima Light (3)	140	2	5	26	620
Swanson Breakfast Blast Mini Pancakes	300	8	6	51	580

Frozen Waffles:

Aunt Jemima (averages for 1 waffle)	90	3	2	14	250
Aunt Jemima Light (1 waffle)	60	1	2	14	240
Belgian Chef Belgian Waffle (1)	70	1	2	11	230
Downyflake (averages for 2 waffles)	170	4	4	31	590
Eggo "Common Sense" Oat Bran Waffle (1)	110	4	3	16	220
Eggo Mini Waffles (4)	90	3	2	14	190
Food Club Waffles (2)	210	5	5	36	720
Kelloggs Special K & Whole Grain (1)	80	0	3	16	130

Frozen French Toast:

Aunt Jemima (averages of all varieties)					
2 pieces	230	7	9	36	310

GRANOLA

Regular granola cereals and bars tend to have large amounts of fat-5 to 6 grams worth per ounce or bar. Scan the store shelves to locate those brands you can eat more freely, including the following:

Kelloggs or Quaker low-fat granola
Kelloggs low-fat granola bars
Health Valley fat-free granola and/or bars
Fat-free granola sold in bulk at natural food stores
Fibar bars
Quaker granola bars having 3 grams fat or less per serving

MARGARINES: Includes most national brands.

Preferred for spreading: Liquid-based oils having less than or equal to 8 grams of total fat and no more than 2 grams of saturated fat per tablespoon.

Preferred for baking: Liquid-based oils above 8 grams fat, yet no more than 2 grams of saturated fat per serving. These work especially well in baking since there is less water added. Since fat content of baked goods (eg. cookies, cakes, pies) is high, watch portion sizes.

Preferred for Spreading:
    Country Crock Spread
    Diet Mazola
    Fleischmann's Light Stick
    Fleischmann's Light Tub
    Food Club Spread
    I Can't Believe It's Not Butter Light Tub
    Land o' Lakes Country Morning Blend Light Tub
    Mazola Extra Light Spread
    Promise Extra Light Stick
    Promise Ultra
    Smart Beat Tub
    Weight Watchers Extra Light Spread

Preferred for Baking:
    Fleischmann's Stick
    Food Club Stick
    Kroger Corn Oil Stick
    Land o' Lakes Spread with Sweet Cream
    Mazola Stick
    Promise Stick
    Any of the squeeze margarines

BREAKFAST MEAT OPTIONS
Limit 1-2 ounces per serving

We truly are a land of meat lovers -- it is our greatest source of protein as well as fat. *Ground hamburger is the single biggest contributor of fat to the national diet!* Other high fat meats more common to breakfast are regular sausage, bacon, fatty beef steaks and pork chops, and certain fast food breakfast meat sandwiches.

Regular bacon and sausage are breakfast favorites. Reduced-fat alternatives such as turkey bacon and turkey sausage can have up to 33% less fat than their regular counterparts, and contain between 1-2 teaspoons of fat/serving. Still, have them no more than twice a week.

Here are some acceptable lower fat meat selections:
    Lean ham (at least 95% fat free by weight)
    Turkey sausage (look for ones at least 85% fat free by weight
      and have it no more than twice a week)
    Pork loin chops, fat trimmed before cooking
    Chicken or turkey breast, skinless
    TURKEY CHORIZO (see page 186)
    COUNTRY SAUSAGE (see page 185)
    Water-packed tuna (1/4 - 1/2 cup)
    Shrimp (once or twice a week)

Table 16: Low-fat Commercially Prepared Muffins

For your "pro-carb" enjoyment, most of these muffins have about 3-4 grams protein and 25-30 grams carbohydrate.

Item	Serving Size	Cal.	Fat (g)	Sodium (mg)
READY-TO-EAT MUFFINS:				
Hostess Lights Cinnamon Crumb Cake	2 oz.	150	1	190
Entenmann's Fat-Free Muffins, All Varieties	2 oz.	140	less than1	115
FROZEN MUFFINS:				
Pepperidge Farm Wholesome Choice Corn Muffin	1.9 oz.	150	3	190
Weight Watchers Harvest Honey Bran	2.5 oz.	160	4	150
Weight Watchers Blueberry	2.5 oz.	170	5	220
Weight Watchers Banana Nut	2.5 oz.	170	5	250
MUFFIN MIXES:				

Values are for prepared product with whole milk and egg. Drop the calories by 5 and fat by 1 gram a serving if you use skim milk and egg substitute.

Item	Serving Size	Cal.	Fat (g)	Sodium (mg)
Martha White Double Blueberry	1/12	120	3	190
Food Club Wild Blueberry	1/12	120	4	170
Betty Crocker Apple Cinnamon	1/12	120	4	140
Betty Crocker Regular Wild Blueberry	1/12	120	4	140
Betty Crocker Light Wild Blueberry	1/12	70	.6	140
Pillsbury Lovin' Lites Blueberry				

(mixed with water-no milk)	1/12	100	1	160
Duncan Hines Blueberry	1/12	120	3	185
Arrowhead Mills Wheat Bran	1.75	135	3.5	165
Kroger Wild Blueberry	1/12	105	3	300
Krusteaz Fat Free Wild Blueberry	1/11	130	0	260
Krusteaz Fat Free Apple Cinnamon	1/11	130	0	310

Ready-to-Eat Muffin Selection Tips

Some muffins are to breakfast what cheesecake is to dinner. Munch a muffin at Dunkin Donuts and guess what? You may have ingested at least 10 grams of fat. To determine whether a muffin can fit comfortably into the meal plan, ask for nutrition information whenever possible. McDonald's prides itself on their fat-free muffins, two of which pro-carb connect with lowfat milk and juice.

If the facts remain elusive, understand that the larger the muffin, the more fat and calories. Stick with muffins that are no larger than 2.5 - 3 inches in diameter (the size of a small apple), and have no more than two at a time. It never hurts to split the heftier ones with a companion. Keep the flavors basic, like blueberry, raisin, banana, apple, or bran. Those with nuts, cheese, or chocolate could wreak havoc on the waistline!

Table 17: Recipe Modification Guidelines

WHEN YOUR RECIPE CALLS FOR:	USE THESE LOW-FAT ALTERNATIVES:
Greasing pans with butter, shortening or margarine	Vegetable cooking spray
Butter	Light tub or light stick margarine, or an oil such as corn or canola. Added fat can usually be decreased by 1/3 to 1/2. Use butter-flavored granules like Butter Buds and Molly McButter in hot, moist foods like scrambled

	eggs and oatmeal. Applesauce or cooked, pureed prunes can substitute for 1/2 the fat in some baked recipes.
Whole milk	Lowfat or skim milk
Heavy cream or Sour cream	Canned evaporated skim milk, low-fat or or fat-free yogurt, cottage cheese or buttermilk. Mix together 1 part oil to 3 parts milk for a cream substitute that is lower in saturated fat.
Shortening, lard, bacon, and chicken fat	Small amounts of oil or light margarine. Use vegetable cooking spray for frying and coating baking pans. Bits of lean ham, turkey breast, onion, bell pepper and spices can be used to season beans and vegetables.
Regular cheese	Low-fat or fat-free cheeses (see "Shopping Guide" page 221)
Whole Eggs	Egg whites or egg substitute (2 egg whites or 1/4 CUP egg substitute equals 1 whole egg).
Sugar	Reduce sugar by 1/3 to 1/2 in baked good recipes; saccharin (eg Sweet 'n Low) can substitute for up to 1/3 of the sugar in recipes that require baking, and Sunette (eg Sweet One) can replace up to 1/2 the sugar a recipe needs.

GUIDE FOR EATING BREAKFAST AWAY FROM HOME

We all deserve a restaurant splurge once in a while. To help ease the load, try some of these tips:

*   Share portions with your companion.

*   Go to places where there is no "all you can eat" promotion.

*   Munch on a low-fat "something or other" beforehand (eg. noodle soup, fresh fruit, carrot sticks, etc.).

*   Exercise before departing to your destination of gluttony.

A Word on Fast Food Breakfasts

Fast food restaurants often use regular sausage and bacon in their breakfast sandwiches. With over 30 grams of fat, the McDonald's biscuit, sausage, and egg sandwich is representative of just how bad it can get. This doesn't mean it's taboo -- just consider it as an occasional luxury (less than once a week). Have one more often if you:

*   Hold added butter or margarine whenever possible.

*   Say "no" to the cheese.

*   Choose English muffins or hamburger buns instead of biscuits or   croissants.

*   Opt for Canadian bacon and ham over the bacon and sausage.

The McDonald's Egg McMuffin is one of the lowest-fat fast food breakfast sandwiches at 11 grams (only 7 grams without the cheese). Burger King has a bagel with ham, egg, and cheese (at select stores) that comes in second at 15 fat grams. McDonald's breakfast burrito (available in some stores) ranks third at 17 grams. Having any of these sandwiches once or twice per week shouldn't be a problem, particularly if you decide to cut out the cheese.

What About Steak for Breakfast?

Besides fast food sandwiches, heavily marbled, untrimmed steaks are also popular. With at least 12-15 grams of fat a serving, fitting them into your fat gram budget can be a burden. Eat these meats rarely, if ever. If you just can't resist, please be wary, because restaurants tend to serve more than 3-4 times the recommended portion size (1-2 ounces). Here are some tried and true tips for ordering breakfast meats at restaurants:

*   Ask fat to be trimmed before cooking. If not, do so when it reaches the table.

*   If steak is ordered, cut it in half and share with friends, or bring the rest home for leftovers.

*   Fill the plate with carbohydrate-laden bread and fruit and small portions of meat.

*   Skip the cream or brown gravy. Use steak sauce or picante salsa instead.

For breakfast, a modest limit of 1-2 ounces of meat is important, especially if more is on the menu for lunch or dinner. Dishes like omelets, casseroles, and sandwiches act as meat extenders so you can more easily stay within the total daily recommendation of 6 ounces or less.

Here are some other ideas on acceptable breakfast choices when eating out. These items more closely meet NCEP guidelines for 30% calories from fat (although some dishes may slightly exceed this level):

Table 18: Acceptable Breakfast Choices When Eating Out

FAST FOOD:

McDonald's Egg McMuffin or
    Breakfast Burrito
McDonald's Pancakes
English Muffin (dry)
Jack in the Box Breakfast Jack
Burger King Bagel, Ham, and Egg
    Sandwich (at selected stores)
Wheat or White Toast
Fat-Free Muffins

Fresh Fruit or Juice
Lowfat or Skim milk
Dry Cereal

FULL SERVICE:

Eggbeater Omelets
Scrambled Egg Whites
Poached Egg
Canadian Bacon
Lean Ham
Turkey Bacon
Turkey, Chicken, or Veal Sausage
Cottage Cheese
Pancakes or Waffles

Bagels, Toast, English Muffins
Fruit Kolaches
Dry or Cooked Cereals
Fresh Fruit or Juice
Lowfat or Skim Milk

Table 19: Low Fat Breakfast Substitutes

Instead of this	Choose this	Fat Grams Saved
Cake doughnut	Bagel	8
Whole milk	2% milk	3
2% milk	Skim milk	5
1 slice bacon	1 slice ham	2
Sausage biscuit	Egg McMuffin	10

2 slices French toast
(unknown preparation)   2 medium pancakes   7

Mindful diners should choose these toppings or spreads for pancakes, waffles, or French toast:

* Small amounts of whipped margarine or butter (no more than a 1-2 teaspoons per serving)
* Fat free or light cream cheese (no more than 2 tablespoons of the latter)
* 3-4 whole or 1 tablespoon chopped nuts or peanut butter
* Jam, preserves, syrups
* Sliced fresh or canned fruit
* Nonfat or lowfat yogurt
* Applesauce

Breakfast Seasoning Tips
Here are seasonings that can complement various breakfast foods --

Lean Meats and Eggs: Allspice, basil, bay leaves, caraway seeds, chives, curry powder, dill, garlic, ginger, lemon juice, dry mustard, nutmeg, onion, paprika, parsley, rosemary, sage, savory, thyme and tumeric.

Cooked Cereals and Grains: Allspice, cinnamon, nutmeg, vanilla or almond extracts.

Canned and Cooked Fruit: Allspice, vanilla, peppermint or almond extracts, cinnamon, ginger, mace and nutmeg.

Even if you don't currently suffer from high blood pressure, do try to stay within the safe and recommended sodium levels (1100-3300 mg a day). The seasonings listed above are splendid salt substitutes.

FOOD BUYING TIPS AND HINTS

Planning ahead is profitable when spending that hard-earned money. Refer to the "WHAT'S FOR BREAKFAST?" shopping guides when composing a grocery list. A well-thought-out list will keep the pantry stocked and restrain impulse buying.

Clipping coupons enables "pre-selection" of foods that are within both monetary and fat budgets. The coupons in newspapers, magazines, and on food packages can introduce a wealth of healthy breakfast foods. Take a calculator along when shopping to determine percent of calories from fat.

Don't shop when hungry. This reduces the temptation to buy more food than needed, particularly convenience items. A morning shopper should go after breakfast.

Purchase foods that require some preparation. For example, instead of buying ready-to-eat coffee cake, bake it from scratch. That way the amount of fat, sodium and calories can be reduced, and the final product will likely cost less.

Beware of those sections in the store where the majority of foods are high in fat. The in-store bakery area is a good example. Detour if at all possible, because out of sight is hopefully out of stomach! Concentrate instead on the fresh produce, dairy, frozen food, cereal aisles, and the bread section to expand your breakfast horizons.

Don't shop when rushed. The more hurried a store trip, the more likely that convenient, high-fat foods wind up in the shopping basket.

RESTRUCTURING THE PANTRY

No, not major remodeling--just restocking with healthful, tasty food. Provision the pantry and refrigerator with a basic breakfast stash:

REFRIGERATOR/FREEZER:

*   Egg substitutes that contain no fat (Fleischmann's Eggbeaters® is our favorite)
*   Whole eggs (eat yolks 4 times a week or less)
*   Frozen pancakes and waffles
*   Two low-fat frozen breakfast entrees (see page 227 for selections)
*   Turkey bacon, turkey sausage (once or twice a week pleasures), lean ham or Canadian bacon (at least 95% fat free as indicated on the nutrition label)
*   Any of the WHAT'S FOR BREAKFAST? recipe leftovers!!!
*   The WHAT'S FOR BREAKFAST? Biscuit Mix (page 184)
*   Light tub and/or stick margarine
*   Light or fat-free cheeses, including cream cheese, ricotta, farmer, cheddar, swiss, and cottage cheese (2% fat or less)
*   Fresh fruits that need refrigeration (oranges, kiwi, melon, or seasonal berries)
*   2-3 types of 100% fruit juices (with 100% vitamin C--check label)
*   1-2 vegetable juices (tomato, carrot, V-8, etc.)
*   Carrots, celery, onions, potatoes, roma tomatoes (because they last longer than the salad tomato variety)
*   Lowfat or skim milk

PANTRY:

* Whole grain bread
* Two ready-to-eat and one hot cereal
* Fat-free or low-fat bran or English muffins
* The WHAT'S FOR BREAKFAST? Pancake and Muffin Mixes (page 182-184)
* Commercial light biscuit mix (if you don't have the WHAT'S FOR BREAKFAST? Biscuit Mix handy)
* Evaporated skim milk
* Fat-free or light coffee creamer
* Maple and fruit breakfast syrups, regular or sugar-free (natural ones taste best)
* Jam, jelly, or preserves (preferably sugar-free)
* Natural peanut butter (Laura Scudder® or Smucker's® are examples) or light peanut butter
* Fresh fruits that don't need refrigeration, like apples, bananas, or pears
* Canned fruits (in their own juices)
* Unsweetened applesauce
* Dried fruit like raisins, apricots, or apples
* Spices such as cinnamon, nutmeg, and cloves
* Regular and decaffeinated coffee or tea
* Cocoa powder

Note: Put the nuts, chips, and candy out of reach. An arrangement of fresh fruit in an attractive basket or bowl can act as an effective diversion.

Appendices

A change of heart is the essence of all other change, and it is brought about by a re-education of the mind.

Emmeline Pethick-Lawrence

Appendices

APPENDIX A: Determination of Body Frame Size:

Estimate your frame size by using wrist circumference and height. Follow steps 1-4:

1. Use right wrist for measurement.

2. Place soft measuring tape around the smallest part of the wrist, in front of the wrist-bone. If the values on the measuring tape are in inches, convert to centimeters (cm) by multiplying by 2.54.

3. Take height in inches and multiply it by 2.54 for conversion to centimeters.

4. Divide height in centimeters by wrist circumference in centimeters. This determines Body Frame Reference Size:

Height in centimeters divided by wrist circumference in centimeters = Body Frame Reference Size.

Compare the Body Frame Reference Size to what is indicated in the following table to get an estimated frame size:

Men	Frame Size	Women	Frame Size
10.4 cm or greater	small	11.0 cm or greater	small
9.6 to 10.4	medium	10.1 to 11.0	medium
9.6 or less	large	10.1 or less	large

For instance, for a man with a wrist measurement of 15 centimeters and a height is 165 centimeters (about 65 inches), divide 165 by 15. The answer is 11. According to the chart, he has a small frame.

Source: Grant, Anne, and Susan DeHoog. NUTRITIONAL ASSESSMENT AND SUPPORT, 4TH EDITION. Seattle: Anne Grant and Susan Dehoog, 1991.

APPENDIX B: Desirable Weight Ranges in Pounds

MEN

Height (inches)	Small Frame	Medium Frame	Large Frame
62	128-134	131-141	138-150
63	130-136	133-143	140-153
64	132-138	135-145	142-156
65	134-140	137-148	144-160
66	136-142	139-151	146-164
67	138-145	142-154	149-168
68	140-148	145-157	152-172
69	142-151	148-160	155-176
70	144-154	151-163	158-180
71	146-157	154-166	161-184
72	149-160	157-170	164-188
73	152-164	160-174	168-192
74	155-168	164-178	172-197
75	158-172	167-182	176-202
76	162-176	171-187	181-207

WOMEN

Height (inches)	Small Frame	Medium Frame	Large Frame
58	102-111	109-121	118-131
59	103-113	111-123	120-134
60	104-115	113-126	122-137
61	106-118	115-129	125-140
62	108-121	118-132	128-143
63	111-124	121-135	131-147
64	114-127	124-138	134-151
65	117-130	127-141	137-155
66	120-133	130-144	140-159
67	123-136	133-147	143-163
68	126-139	136-150	146-167
69	129-142	139-153	149-170
70	132-145	142-156	152-173
71	135-151	148-162	158-179

These assume 1 inch heels and indoor clothing weighing 5 pounds. Tables from Metropolitan Life Insurance Co. 1983. Rough guidelines only, see a physician or dietetian for more specific weight information based on age.

Nutrition Nugget: Setting Realistic Weight Goals

In our relentless quest for thinness, many of us fail to realize that maintaining a stable weight level can be just as important as losing it. Dietitians frequently counsel middle-aged female patients who would like to lose 10 or 20 pounds, even though they look great and are in good health. In reality, they want to look the same as they did 20 years ago. Radical programs touting crash dieting and/or pill popping seem the quickest means to this end. Because this regiment can't be endured forever, the pounds creep back. The cycle of "quick fix" dieting goes on endlessly in response to the rising numbers on the scale.

These "rollercoaster rides" are NOT a good idea. When denied sustenance, the body fights back by becoming even more conservative with its fat reserves. Just as turning down the thermostat saves energy, the body does the same thing with its metabolic rate. The same 10 pounds lost a year ago will probably be twice as hard to drop now!

Do a self-evaluation: Is it necessary to drop pounds, or maintain what's already there? A physician can help with this decision. In either case, lifestyle changes such as healthy breakfasts, scaling back portion sizes, and regular exercise should do the trick. If a weight loss program is desired, find one that is affordable and offers maintenance classes with behavior modification strategies (to help keep the weight off). For more assistance, consult with a registered dietitian on planning an individualized weight control strategy.

APPENDIX C: Determining Caloric Need

Building a healthy breakfast requires learning about which foods are the best providers of the nutrients we need, while keeping total calories in check. Calories from the three major energy-supplying nutrients (carbohydrate, protein, and fat) have two places to go--either to perform their specific functions or be stored as body fat.

Once caloric energy from either carbohydrate, protein, or dietary fat converts to body fat, losing it is very difficult as we well know! The body stockpiles fat and taps into it only when supplementary energy is required. Because the human body (especially the female) acts as a "fat storehouse," physical activity is essential to rid the body of excess fat.

Along with physical activity, the timing of meals is important for weight control (as discussed in Chapter 1, page 6). To discover where calories are coming from, in addition to when they are eaten, write down everything consumed for three days, paying close attention to the amounts. Don't make any changes in what you normally eat at this point. Use a notebook or a plain sheet of paper to record the time eaten (eg. 9:00 AM, 2:00 PM, etc.), food ingested, along with the amount (make as many forms as needed to record all three days). Make sure to clearly separate meals eaten by skipping a line between each meal. Obtain a reliable calorie and fat counter from the library or bookstore (see suggestions below) and add up the calories and fat for each meal. At times it may not be possible to get your quantities to precisely match the values in the calorie/fat counting books. If so, don't worry--just make a good estimate.

Recommended Calorie and Fat Counting Books:
THE COMPLETE BOOK OF FOOD COUNTS by Corinne T. Neltzer.
FOOD AND FITNESS GUIDE by University of Minnesota.
FOOD VALUES OF PORTIONS OF PORTIONS COMMONLY USED by Jean A. Pennington.

Sometimes a person is unable to measure food (eg. at a restaurant, party, etc.). When these situations occur, do the best appraisal possible, then add an extra 30% to the calorie (and fat) value of the whole meal to account for underestimation. For instance, if approximating 800 calories from a church supper, one probably ate closer to 1040 calories (800 X .30 = 240. 800 + 240 = 1040).

Next, sum up the calorie and fat totals for each day. If more than 1/2 of the total calories, (or a 1/3 of daily fat goals, see APPENDIX F) for at least two days are eaten at supper and beyond, it is TOO MUCH. These calories will most likely be stored as fat--particularly if the late afternoon and evening are the least active parts of the day. Calories eaten earlier than this are more likely to be burned as fuel, thus preventing weight gain. By now, the value of morning dining for weight control should be clear. The goal is to start eating less later and more earlier.

How Many Calories Do We Need?

Since we've established the importance of calorie distribution throughout the day, determining daily caloric requirements is the next step. First, determine body frame size using Appendix A. After calculating frame size, compare current weight with the recommendations in Appendix B. This will determine whether a person is at, above, or below desirable weight. Next, match the weight and activity level with one of the following nine categories, and multiply current weight by the underlined figure. The resulting number is the calories required to maintain present weight.

At desirable weight:

a)   Sedentary to light activity (exercises no more than 1-2 times per week, less than 30 minutes per session), MULTIPLY WEIGHT BY 13. Example: Alice weighs 155 pounds, and never exercises. The calories needed to maintain her weight are 2015 per day (155 x 13 = 2015). Please note: This category includes those who exercise 1-2 times per week for more than 30 minutes per session

b)   Moderately active (exercises 3-4 times weekly, 30 minutes or more per session), MULTIPLY WEIGHT BY 15. Example: Penny weighs 120 pounds, and exercises 4 times per week. The calories needed to maintain her weight are 1800 per day (120 x 15 = 1800).

c)   Very active (exercising 5-7 times per week at least 30 minutes per session), MULTIPLY WEIGHT BY 18. Example: Bill weighs 175 pounds, and works out daily. The calories needed to maintain his weight are 3150 per day (175 x 18 = 3150).

Above desirable weight:

a) Sedentary to light activity, MULTIPLY WEIGHT BY 10. Example: Jane weighs 200 pounds, and is sedentary. The calories needed to maintain her weight are 2000 per day (2000 x 10 = 2000).

b) Moderately active, MULTIPLY WEIGHT BY 13. Example: Sally weighs 170 pounds and is moderately active. The calories needed maintain her weight are 2210 per day (170 x 13 = 2210).

c) Very active, MULTIPLY WEIGHT BY 15. Example: Larry weighs 235 pounds, and is very active. The calories needed to maintain his weight are 3525 per day (235 x 15 = 3525).

Below desirable weight:

a) Sedentary to light activity, MULTIPLY WEIGHT BY 13. Example: Wendy weighs 98 pounds, and is inactive. The calories needed to maintain her weight are 1274 per day (98 x 13 = 1274).

b) Moderately active, MULTIPLY WEIGHT BY 18. Example: Ted weighs 120 pounds, and is moderately active. The calories needed to maintain his weight are 1800 per day (120 x 15 = 1800).

c) Very active, MULTIPLY WEIGHT BY 20. Example: Kelly weighs 110 pounds, and is very active. The calories needed to maintain her weight are 2200 per day (110 x 20 = 2200).

Adjusting calories is one way to reduce or increase weight. Each pound of fat has 3,500 calories. To lose one pound in a week, a 500 calorie deficit per day is required (500 x 7 days = 3500). A 750 calorie cutback allows for 1 1/2 pounds to disappear in a week (750 x 7 days = 5250, which is 1 1/2 times greater than 3,500). Don't get too overzealous, because 1-2 pounds of weight loss/gain per week is the recommended limit.

Fill in the following blanks to evaluate your personal calorie goals for weight control.

Number of calories I currently consume is: _____ per day.

If I choose to lose 1-2 pounds per week, I must decrease my daily calories by 500-1000 per day.

_____ calories is the number of calories needed to achieve my weight control goal.

Distributing Needed Calories At Breakfast And Throughout The Day

Since mornings are an active time for most people, breakfast should comprise a substantial portion of daily calories. Have at least 25-35% of total calories at breakfast. For instance, if the daily calorie target is 1500, 25% of this total is 375 calories (1500 x .25 = 375). 35% of total daily calories is 525. Thus, the range of breakfast calories for a 1500 calorie diet is 375-525 calories.

APPENDIX D: Determining Daily Protein Needs

1   Identify daily caloric needs (see APPENDIX C)
2.   Multiply this number by .15 and .20 (these numbers represent 15% and 20% respectively) This gives a range of recommended protein calories.
3.   Divide the resulting numbers by 4 to arrive at a range of protein intake in grams (there are 4 calories per gram of protein).

For example, if a person requires 1500 calories per day:

A.   1500 x .15 = 225
   1500 x .20 = 300

B.   225 divided by 4 = 56.25 (or 56 g)
   300 divided by 4 = 75 grams

The range of protein intake is anywhere between 56-75 grams per day. STRIVE FOR 15 GRAMS OF PROTEIN AT BREAKFAST FOR A PRO-CARB CONNECTION (see page 73)!

APPENDIX E: Determining Daily Carbohydrate Needs

1. Identify caloric needs (see APPENDIX C)
2. Multiply this number by .50 and .60 (these numbers represent 50% and 60% respectively). This gives you a range of required carbohydrate calories.
3. Divide the resulting numbers by 4 to arrive at a range of carbohydrate intake in grams (there are 4 calories per gram of carbohydrate)

For example, if you require 1800 calories per day:

A. 1800 X .50 = 900 Carbohydrate calories   B. 900 divided by 4 = 225 g Carbo.
    1800 X .60 = 1080 Carbohydrate calories   1080 divided by 4 = 270 g Carbo.

The range of carbohydrate intake is anywhere between 225 and 270 grams per day. STRIVE FOR 40 GRAMS OF CARBOHYDRATE AT BREAKFAST FOR A SOUND PRO-CARB CONNECTION (see page 65).

APPENDIX F: Calculating Daily Fat Needs

To start, determine daily caloric requirement (see APPENDIX C). In the chart on the next page, match calories listed in the first column with the corresponding fat gram goal in the second column.

Daily Calories = Daily Fat Gram Goal

1200 calories per day = 40 grams of fat per day
1500 calories per day = 50 grams of fat per day
1800 calories per day = 60 grams of fat per day
2000 calories per day = 70 grams of fat per day
2500 calories per day = 83 grams of fat per day

How were these fat gram values derived? Each calorie level was multiplied by .3 (which represents 30%--the recommended upper limit for percentage of calories coming from fat goal as outlined in the National Cholesterol Education Program guidelines discussed on page 000. The resulting number was divided by 9, which is the number of calories in a gram of fat.

To calculate *daily* fat gram goals based on daily calories not listed in the chart above, do the following:

1. Multiply the total calories by .3 (which represents 30%)
2. Divide this number by 9 (number of calories in a gram of fat)
3. The resulting number is the fat gram requirement per day.

Find an abbreviated roster of fat gram values in APPENDIX I (AVERAGE NUTRIENT VALUES OF TYPICAL BREAKFAST FOODS). The recommended calorie and fat counter books in APPENDIX C offer a more complete listing of fat gram values. Awareness of fat content is the definitive path to a clearer understanding of dietary options. For instance, a fast food biscuit, sausage, and egg sandwich can contain a whopping 24-36 grams of fat, sabotaging one's best intentions at fat restriction. Without this clarity, making sound decisions on appropriate food choices at breakfast (or any other meal) is more difficult.

Don't agonize if fat gram goals are exceeded occasionally. Compensate by eating less fat the remainder of that day or over the next few days. Instead of eliminating best loved foods, just eat them less often.

Saturated Fat Intake Goals

According to the National Cholesterol Education Program, no more than 10% of total calories should come from saturated fat (the average for Americans is 12-13%). In other words, less than 1/3 of total daily fat should come from saturates. For instance, for a 50 gram total fat goal per day, no more than 17 grams of saturated fat should be ingested (50 X .33=17). Read why restricting saturated fat is so important on page 27.

Here is a concise way of examining saturated fat gram goals at several daily calorie levels.

Daily Calorie Level	Saturated Fat Goal (grams)
1200	13
1500	17
1800	20
2000	22
2500	28

For calorie levels not listed, just remove the last zero and divide the resulting number by 9.   Example: 2220 calories
222 divided by 9 = 24.6 (round up to 25)
In applying this information to a morning meal, assume a breakfast total fat goal is no more than 15 grams. The ceiling for saturated fat would be 5 grams (15 x .33 = 5).

APPENDIX G: Nutrition Labeling Information

Because of a strong consumer outcry for change in nutrition labeling standards, the Nutrition Labeling and Education Act (NLEA) was passed in 1990. Its purpose was to overhaul label content, primarily to standardize information and beef up the regulations regarding nutrition claims on manufacturers' edible merchandise. See the next page for an example of the latest version of a nutrition label.

The New Food Label at a Glance

The new food label will carry an up-to-date, easier-to-use nutrition information guide, to be required on almost all packaged foods (compared to about 60 percent of products up till now). The guide will serve as a key to help in planning a healthy diet.*

Serving sizes are now more consistent across product lines, stated in both household and metric measures, and reflect the amounts people actually eat.

New title signals that the label contains the newly required information.

Nutrition Facts

Serving Size ½ cup (114g)

Servings Per Container 4

Amount Per Serving

Calories 90	Calories from Fat 30

	% Daily Value*
Total Fat 3g	**5%**
Saturated Fat 0g	**0%**
Cholesterol 0mg	**0%**
Sodium 300mg	**13%**
Total Carbohydrate 13g	**4%**
Dietary Fiber 3g	**12%**
Sugars 3g	
Protein 3g	

Vitamin A	80%	•	Vitamin C	60%
Calcium	4%	•	Iron	4%

* Percent Daily Values are based on a 2,000 calorie diet. Your daily values may be higher or lower depending on your calorie needs:

	Calories	2,000	2,500
Total Fat	Less than	65g	80g
Sat Fat	Less than	20g	25g
Cholesterol	Less than	300mg	300mg
Sodium	Less than	2,400mg	2,400mg
Total Carbohydrate		300g	375g
Fiber		25g	30g

Calories per gram:

Fat 9   •   Carbohydrate 4   •   Protein 4

Calories from fat are now shown on the label to help consumers meet dietary guidelines that recommend people get no more than 30 percent of their calories from fat.

% Daily Value shows how a food fits into the overall daily diet.

The **list of nutrients** covers those most important to the health of today's consumers, most of whom need to worry about getting too much of certain items (fat, for example), rather than too few vitamins or minerals, as in the past.

The label of larger packages must now tell the number of calories per gram of fat, carbohydrate, and protein.

Daily Values are also something new. Some are maximums, as with fat (65 grams or less); others are minimums, as with carbohydrate (300 grams or more). The daily values for a 2,000- and 2,500-calorie diet must be listed on the label of larger packages. Individuals should adjust the values to fit their own calorie intake.

* This label is only a sample. Exact specifications are in the final rules.
Source: Food and Drug Administration 1993

Nutrition Claims

Manufacturers use eye-catching nutritional claims such as light or lite, free, low, reduced, less, and high to give their products a competitive edge. Here are key nutrition terms and their meanings as defined by the government.

Calorie Free -- less than 5 calories per serving.Lite, Light,
Low Calorie -- 40 calories or less per serving.
Reduced/Less Calorie -- this distinguishes foods having calories per serving reduced by 25% or more.
Light, Lite, Lightly -- has at least one-third less calories or 50% less fat than its counterparts. When describing color, texture, or taste, the particular characteristic MUST be identified. For example, an olive oil bottle must read that it is "light" in color, since no oil as of yet is truly "light" in calories or fat.
Fat Free/No Fat/Nonfat -- no more than 0.5 gram of fat per serving.
Low Fat -- 3 grams of fat or less per serving.
Lowfat (one word) -- refers to milk or milk products that have "some" milk-fat removed. Milk percentages, such as 1% and 2%, describes the fat volume, not fat calories. (*Note that "lowfat" is one word when describing milk. It becomes two words when associated with other foods). Inspect milk labels carefully for fat content, as they are highly variable. For instance, 2% lowfat milk has 5 grams of fat per cup, while 1/2 percent drops to .5 gram.
Reduced Fat/Less Fat -- at least 25% less fat than its original counterpart.
Saturated Fat Free -- less than 1/2 gram of saturated fat per serving.
Low in Saturated Fat -- the cutoff point for this descriptor is 1 gram saturated fat per serving and not more than 15% of calories from saturated fat.
Reduced/Less Saturated Fat -- at least 25% less saturated fat than its original counterpart, with a minimum reduction of 1 gram saturated fat per serving.
Cholesterol Free/No Cholesterol -- less than 2 milligrams of cholesterol AND 2 grams or less of saturated fat per serving. Other analogous terms are "no cholesterol" and "zero cholesterol."
Low Cholesterol/Low in Cholesterol -- no more than 20 milligrams of cholesterol and 2 grams of saturated fat per serving.

Reduced/Less Cholesterol -- cholesterol is cut by 25% or more. The reduction must be at least 20 milligrams per serving.

Lean/Extra Lean (for meat and poultry) -- "lean" describes meat or poultry products with no more than 10 grams of fat, 4 grams of saturated fat, and 95 milligrams of cholesterol per 100 grams cooked weight (about 3 1/2 ounces). "Extra lean" meat contains less than 5 grams of fat, less than 2 grams of saturated fat, and less than 95 milligrams of cholesterol per 100 grams cooked weight.

Sugar Free -- less than 1/2 gram of total sugar per serving.

Reduced/Less Sugar -- at least 25% less sugar than its original counterpart.

Sodium/Salt Free -- no more than 5 milligrams of sodium per serving.

Very Low Sodium -- no more than 35 milligrams of sodium per serving.

Low Sodium -- 140 milligrams of sodium or less per serving.

Reduced/Less Sodium -- at least 25% less sodium than its original counterpart.

Light in Sodium or "Lite in Sodium" -- 50% less sodium than its original counterpart.

More, Fortified, Enriched, or Added -- these words describe a food that contains at least 10% more of the Daily Value (see page 255) for protein, fiber, vitamins, or minerals than does a comparable equivalent.

Contact the following agencies for more information on nutrition labels or for answers regarding food and nutrition:

American Dietetic Association Consumer Nutrition Hotline
at #800-366-1655

FDA/USDA Food Labeling Education Information Center
at #301-504-5719   FAX #301-504-6409

APPENDIX H: Coffee, Caffeine and Creamers

For many of us, coffee is an indispensable part of our wakeup ritual. Americans drink an average of 3-5 cups throughout the day. Several studies have indicted coffee as a stimulus in raising blood cholesterol. However, these trials are often not controlled for other habits. The results could be attributed to smoking, skipping breakfast, and poor diet--not coffee itself.

One of the few studies that took into account lifestyle factors was by Fried et. al. reported in 1992. It involved 100 men who drank varying amounts of filtered coffee (filtered means a one-time passage of hot water through the coffee and filter). Findings did show very minor increases in both LDL (bad cholesterol) and HDL (good cholesterol) with 3 cups a day. Because both fractions were elevated, the risk of heart disease wasn't affected.

Other research describes a strong link between blood cholesterol levels and drinking boiled coffee, a common preparation method in Northern European countries (boiled refers to coffee grounds that have been cooked in boiling water, then strained). A 1989 study conducted in the Netherlands by Bak and Grobbee involved 107 participants who were all in good health and had normal blood cholesterol levels. For nine weeks, half the group drank 4 to 6 cups of boiled coffee, while the other half drank the same amount of filtered coffee. Boiled coffee raised total cholesterol levels by 10 percent, while filtered coffee had no effect.

Some unidentified component in coffee that is not trapped by the coffee filter is the probable offender. Oily substances found in certain types of coffee beans have been implicated, but not enough research has been done to reach a definitive conclusion.

Heavy intake of caffeine (over 9 cups of coffee per day)has been accused of being the cause of high cholesterol and heart attacks. Research has been conflicting--some studies show a slightly increased cardiovascular risk with drinking regular coffee, while other studies do not.

Coffee drinking has also been implicated in the elevation of blood pressure, with caffeine again deemed the instigator. Several studies done in the last 15 years showed small upward swings in systolic and diastolic readings with intakes of three or more cups.

So, what can be concluded from the conflicting research cited thus far? Coffee (especially boiled) can adversely affect cholesterol and blood pressure in certain individuals, but more studies are needed for verification. As with everything else, moderation is always the best policy. Confine your intake to 3-4 cups (24-32 fluid ounces) of either regular or decaffeinated coffee.

Drinking more than 4 cups of coffee per day? Try alternating coffee with other beverages such as water, herbal tea, and unsweetened juices. Or use small coffee cups instead of large mugs. Consider CAFE AU LAIT, which is half coffee, half hot milk (see page 180). MEXICAN HOT COCOA (see page 180) may convert even the most die-hard coffee lover.

What Is Known About Caffeine:

* Caffeine can affect prenatal bone development, and also lead to low birth weight. This means a suggested maximum of 200-300 milligrams (mg) per day (about 16-24 fluid ounces of coffee) for pregnant women.

* There is no evidence that caffeine induces cancer, heart disease, or hypertension. As noted earlier, it can lead to temporary swings in blood pressure or heart rate, but this doesn't happen to everyone.

* Caffeine acts as a diuretic, meaning the more caffeinated beverages you drink, the more visits to the bathroom you will make!

* Speaking of bathroom trips, too much caffeine may cause excessive amounts of calcium to be excreted in the urine, increasing the risk of osteoporosis.

* Caffeine has not been linked to breast cancer, but it can cause breasts to feel full, sore, and tender around menstruation time.   A woman suffering from this problem should reduce caffeine to 200 mg or less per day.

* Athletes should limit pre-competition caffeine intake to no more than 120 mg (equal to one cup of coffee) so as to retain fluids   for the event. Although it is believed by some researchers that caffeine can preserve glycogen stores, its effect is most likely temporary.

If you choose to use less caffeine, do so gradually to diminish any disagreeable side effects like anxiety, headaches, or depression.

Breakfast appetites can be dulled by too much caffeine. By lunchtime, you end up famished, and the temptation for mega fat and sugar indulgences can be irresistible.

Table 20: Caffeine Content of Various Beverages

Beverage	Amount	Caffeine (mg)
Coffee	1 cup brewed	137
Coffee	1 cup instant	76
Tea	1 cup brewed	72
Herbal tea	1 cup	0
Sodas containing caffeine	12 ounces	40-55
Hot cocoa	1 cup	6
Chocolate milk	1 cup	8

Creamers

The lightest of the coffee whiteners are low-fat dairy products. Opt for skim milk, canned evaporated skim milk, or non-fat dry milk powder, especially if drinking more than a cup of coffee a day. Many complain that by themselves, these low-fat options do not provide enough richness or taste. A suggestion is to mix 2 teaspoons of non-fat dry milk powder with 1/2 cup evaporated skim milk. Add as much of this mixture to your coffee as desired.

Store-bought powdered and liquid creamers now come in fat-free and light varieties. They should carry no more than one gram of fat per teaspoon, and contain acceptable oils like canola or corn oil. Fat from light creamers can accumulate, so watch the serving size --about 1-2 teaspoons per cup.

Give this CREAMY MOCHA JAVA recipe a try. Simply drop a 1/4 cup of nonfat or low-fat chocolate frozen yogurt into a cup of hot coffee. Add a two-second spray of light aerosol whipped topping and enjoy!

APPENDIX I: Breakfast Food Nutrient Values

Table 21: Average Nutrient Values Of Typical Breakfast Foods

Food	Protein (g)	Carbohydrate (g)	Fat (g)	Sat Fat (g)	Calories	Chol (mg)
a) Starch/Bread:	3	15	trace	---	800	
1/2 cup cereal, grain, potato, or pasta OR 1 slice bread, 1/2 bagel or English muffin, 1 corn tortilla						
b) Starch/Bread:	2-3	15	3-5	2	125	15-25
Small biscuit, cornbread (2-ounce piece), plain muffin, flour tortilla, 2 5-inch pancakes OR a 5 1/2 inch waffle						
c) Starch/Bread:	2-3	15	12	4	200-220	15-25
Croissant, danish, doughnut, large biscuit						
Vegetables:	2	5	0	0	25	0
1 cup raw or 1/2 cup cooked						

Food	Protein (g)	Carbohydrate (g)	Fat (g)	Sat Fat (g)	Calories	Chol (mg)
Fruit:	1	15	0	0	60	0

1 med. piece whole fruit, eg. apple, orange, etc. OR 1/2 cup fruit pieces, applesauce, or unsweetened juice

Dairy Products:

Food	Protein (g)	Carbohydrate (g)	Fat (g)	Sat Fat (g)	Calories	Chol (mg)
a) 1 cup skim/1/2%	8	12	0-.5	trace	80-90	

milk or nonfat yogurt, or fruit-flavored nonfat yogurt sweetened with aspartame

Food	Protein (g)	Carbohydrate (g)	Fat (g)	Sat Fat (g)	Calories	Chol (mg)
b) 1 cup fruit flavored yogurt, nonfat	8	35-38	0-.5	trace	190	2-4
c) 1 cup 2% milk	8	12	5	2-3	120	15-20

or plain yogurt, or low-fat fruit-flavored yogurt sweetened with aspartame

Food	Protein (g)	Carbohydrate (g)	Fat (g)	Sat Fat (g)	Calories	Chol (mg)
d) 1 cup fruit-flavored yogurt, low-fat	8	35-38	4-5	2-3	220-240	15-20
e) 1 cup whole milk or whole milk yogurt	8	12	8	5	150	33
f) 1 ounce fat-free cheese	8	3	0	0	50	0
g) 2 tablespoons fat-free cream cheese	5	2	0	0	30	0
h) 2 tablespoons light cream cheese	2	trace	3	2	35	10-15
i) 1 ounce light cheese (on average)	8	1	3-6	2-3	90	10-20
j) 1 ounce regular cheese	8	trace	8-10	5-6	100-120	20-30
k) 2 tablespoons fat-free sour cream	2	3	0	0	20	

Food	Protein (g)	Carbohydrate (g)	Fat (g)	Sat Fat (g)	Calories	Chol (mg)
l) 2 tablespoons light sour cream	2	4	1	1	36	10-15
m) 2 tablespoons regular sour cream	1	1	5	3	52	12

Meat: (per ounce)

Food	Protein (g)	Carbohydrate (g)	Fat (g)	Sat Fat (g)	Calories	Chol (mg)
a) **Lean**-- round,	7	0	1-3	1-2	50-60	20-25

loin red meat cuts, poultry (skinless breast), lean ham, whitefish

Food	Protein (g)	Carbohydrate (g)	Fat (g)	Sat Fat (g)	Calories	Chol (mg)
b) **Medium-fat**--	7	0	4-5	2-3	75-80	25-35

chuck, shoulder red meat cuts, oily fish (eg. salmon), ground meat (eg. beef or turkey)

Food	Protein (g)	Carbohydrate (g)	Fat (g)	Sat Fat (g)	Calories	Chol (mg)
c) **High-fat**-- ribs,	7	0	7-8	4-6	100-110	25-35

sausage, poultry (dark meat with skin), fatty ham

Food	Protein (g)	Carbohydrate (g)	Fat (g)	Sat Fat (g)	Calories	Chol (mg)
Egg, 1 whole large	6	---	5	2	75	213
Egg, 1 white or 1/4	3	---	0	0	16	0
Egg substitute, 1/4 cup, fat free	5	1	0	0	25	0
Peanut butter, 1 tablespoon	4	---	8	1-2	95	0
Nuts, 2 tablespoons (eg. walnuts, pecans, almonds)	4	---	10	1-2	90	0

Fat:

Food	Protein (g)	Carbohydrate (g)	Fat (g)	Sat Fat (g)	Calories	Chol (mg)
Oil, 1 tablespoon	---	---	13	p 29	120	0
Butter, 1 tablespoon	---	---	12	---	110	31
Light butter, 1 tablespoon	---	---	6	---	50	30
Margarine, 1 tablespoon, regular stick	---	---	11	2-3	100	0

Food	Protein (g)	Carbohydrate (g)	Fat (g)	Sat Fat (g)	Calories	Chol (mg)
Margarine, 1 tablespoon, regular tub	---	---	10-11	2-3	90-100	0
Margarine, 1 tablespoon, light tub or stick	---	---	7	2	60-70	0
Margarine, 1 tablespoon, extra light	---	---	3-4	.5-1	45-50	0
Coffee cream, non-dairy, regular (1 teaspoon)	---	---	2	1	30	0
Coffee cream, non-dairy, light (1 teaspoon)	---	---	.3	.3	8	0

Adapted from the American Dietetic Association and the American Diabetes Association Exchange Lists, 1989

APPENDIX J: High Sodium Breakfast Foods

Food	Sodium (milligrams)
2 slices Canadian bacon	710
2 strips turkey bacon, cooked	400
1 ounce regular ham (3 gm fat per ounce)	380
1 ounce reduced fat ham (1 gram/ounce)	380
1 ounce regular sausage	350
1 ounce reduced fat AND sodium ham	230
2 strips regular bacon, cooked	200
1/2 cup regular cottage cheese (average)	425
1 ounce (1 slice) American cheese	400
1 English muffin	400
10 soda crackers	300
1 biscuit, from refrigerated dough	250

Corn Flakes®, 1 ounce (1 1/4 cups)	350
Chex® cereal, 1 ounce (2/3 cup)	300
Cheerios®, 1 ounce (1 1/4 cups)	290
Total®, 1 ounce (1 cup)	280
Tomato or V-8® juice, 6 fluid ounces	650

When watching sodium, choose foods with 160 milligrams or less of sodium per serving.

APPENDIX K: Foods With High Fiber Content (3 or more grams per serving)

Food:	Fiber (grams)
Fruits	
Medium size unpeeled fresh pear	4.7
1 cup blueberries	3.9
Medium size unpeeled apple	3.7
1 cup strawberries	3
Vegetables	
Potato, UNPEELED, medium	5
Broccoli, 1 cup raw or cooked	3
Brussels sprouts, 1/2 cup	3
Peas, green, 1/2 cup	3
Pumpkin, canned, 1/2 cup	3
Breads, Cereals, Starches	
All-Bran® with Extra Fiber 1/2 cup	14
Fiber One® 1/2 cup	13
All-Bran® cereal 1/2 cup	8.5
Oat bran, 1/2 cup	5.5
Bran Flakes® cereal 1/2 cup	4.5

Dark breads like rye or pumpernickel per slice	3
Legumes	
Baked beans, 1/2 cup	6
Black-eyed peas, red beans 1/2 cup	4
Lima beans, 1/2 cup	3.5

Notes

[1] R.E. Fried, et al. "The Effect of Filtered Coffee Consumption on Plasma Lipid Levels." JOURNAL OF THE AMERICAN MEDICAL ASSOCIATION 267 (1992): 811-815.

[2] A. Bak, D.E. Grobbee, "The Effect on Serum Cholesterol Levels of Coffee Brewed by Filtering or Boiling." THE NEW ENGLAND JOURNAL OF MEDICINE 321 (1989): 1132-1137.

[3] Don T. Mitchell, "Coffee and Cholesterol: Grounds for Concern?" IT'S YOUR CHOLESTEROL 3 March 1991: 1-4.

[4] P.C. Rosmarin, et al. "Coffee Consumption and Blood Pressure." JOURNAL OF GENERAL INTERNAL MEDICINE 5 (1990): 211-213.

[5] D. Jeong, J.E. Dimsdale, "The Effects of Caffeine on Blood Pressure in the Work Environment." AMERICAN JOURNAL OF HYPERTENSION 3 (1990): 749-753.

[6] Nancy Clark, NANCY CLARK'S SPORTS NUTRITION GUIDEBOOK. Champaign, IL: Leisure Press, 1990.

Recipe Index